DIVINE MOMENTS

Everyday Inspiration from God's Word

DIVINE MOMENTS

Everyday Inspiration
from God's Word

Tyndale House Publishers, Inc.

Carol Stream, Illinois

Visit Tyndale's exciting Web site at www.tyndale.com

TYNDALE, New Living Translation, NLT, the New Living Translation logo, and Tyndale's quill logo are registered trademarks of Tyndale House Publishers, Inc.

Divine Moments: Everyday Inspiration from God's Word

Questions and notes copyright © 2008 by Ronald A. Beers. All rights reserved.

Cover photo copyright © by Photodisc. All rights reserved.

Managing editors: Ronald A. Beers and Amy E. Mason

Contributing writers: V. Gilbert Beers, Rebecca J. Beers, Brian R. Coffey, Jonathan Farrar, Jeffrey Frasier, Jonathan Gray, Shawn A. Harrison, Sandy Hull, Rhonda K. O'Brien, Douglas J. Rumford, Linda Taylor

Designed by Julie Chen

Edited by Michal Needham

Scripture quotations are taken from the *Holy Bible*, New Living Translation, second edition, copyright © 1996, 2004. Used by permission of Tyndale House Publishers, Inc., Carol Stream, Illinois 60188. All rights reserved.

ISBN-13: 978-1-4143-1225-5

ISBN-10: 1-4143-1225-3

Printed in the United States of America

14   13   12   11   10   09   08

7   6   5   4   3   2   1

Introduction

The goal of *Divine Moments* is to help you experience a breakthrough with God, to show you how and where God is at work in your life to get your attention each day. If the Bible is really a blueprint for living, then God, through his Word, should be able to respond to any question you have for him. And he does! As you read the questions and Scripture in this book, it is amazing to see how God's answers to your daily needs are so clear and help you see with "spiritual eyes" how he is trying to break through to you. Sometimes God seems so big and mysterious that you may wonder whether he would truly bother with you. But he loves you personally and is trying to get your attention every day. This little book can help you notice the divine moments when he is trying to show you how much he cares. You can read straight through the book, or you can use it topically when you are looking for God's help in a certain area of life or if you just need more clarity about what God might say about something that is important to you. We pray this little book will be meaningful to you and help you experience many divine moments with God.

—The editors

Abilities

Where do my abilities come from, and how should I use them?

A MOMENT *with* GOD

To those who use well what they are given, even
more will be given, and they will have an abundance.
But from those who do nothing, even what little they
have will be taken away.   MATTHEW 25:29

When someone has been given much, much will be
required in return; and when someone has been
entrusted with much, even more will be required.

LUKE 12:48

Deep within the human spirit lie a longing and a capacity to do wonderful things. Because you are made
in the image of God, you inherited from him the desire to create, to accomplish, to make things happen.
God wouldn't give you these desires without the ability
to carry them out. These abilities are gifts from God
to help you accomplish great things for him and live a
fulfilling life. How you use or misuse them ultimately
determines your quality of life—quality being not
comfort or the accumulation of things, but character,
joy, and lasting satisfaction. Your goal is to first discover your abilities; second, to develop them; and then
channel them toward what is good, helpful, productive, and honoring to God. As you obediently exercise
and develop your abilities, God's purpose for their uses

becomes clear, and you get a glimpse into what God can do through you now and what you will eventually become when you are able to fully utilize your abilities in eternity.

DIVINE PROMISE

IN HIS GRACE, GOD HAS GIVEN US DIFFERENT GIFTS FOR DOING CERTAIN THINGS WELL.

Romans 12:6

Absolutes

MY QUESTIONS *for* GOD

Are there really absolutes in life? And if so, how can I know what they are?

A MOMENT *with* GOD

People may be right in their own eyes, but the LORD examines their heart.   PROVERBS 21:2

In those days Israel had no king; all the people did whatever seemed right in their own eyes.   JUDGES 21:25

If you criticize and judge each other, then you are criticizing and judging God's law. But your job is to obey the law, not to judge whether it applies to you.

                                      JAMES 4:11

*I*magine you've just bought a new cell phone or computer. You can ignore the instructions for using it, and it will still work. But you'll miss many of the great things it was meant to do, and you'll miss much of what you could have enjoyed. Now let's say that instead of ignoring the instructions, you purposely do the opposite of what the manual tells you to do. Now you've got a bigger problem. Your phone or computer will frustrate you every day because nothing will work right.

There's a certain way to get these gadgets to work, and the instruction book tells you what that way is. It's the same with life. The Bible is God's instruction manual for life. God has programmed certain absolutes into the world, and they apply to all people, in all times, and in all places. Ignore God's instructions, and you'll miss much of what God intends for you to enjoy. But go against his instructions, and chances are good that you'll end up hurt, frustrated, and disappointed. That's why it is so important not only to read the Bible and discover God's absolutes but also to live by them. Doing so can make life much smoother, and it will certainly be more fulfilling.

DIVINE PROMISE

ALL SCRIPTURE IS INSPIRED BY GOD AND IS USEFUL TO TEACH US WHAT IS TRUE AND TO MAKE US REALIZE WHAT IS WRONG IN OUR LIVES. IT CORRECTS US WHEN WE ARE WRONG AND TEACHES US TO DO WHAT IS RIGHT.

2 Timothy 3:16

Acceptance

MY QUESTION *for* GOD

Can God really accept me, even after all I've done?

A MOMENT *with* GOD

God showed his great love for us by sending Christ to
die for us while we were still sinners.   ROMANS 5:8

This is a trustworthy saying, and everyone should
accept it: "Christ Jesus came into the world to save
sinners"—and I am the worst of them all.

1 TIMOTHY 1:15

God showed how much he loved us by sending his one
and only Son into the world so that we might have
eternal life through him. This is real love—not that
we loved God, but that he loved us and sent his Son as
a sacrifice to take away our sins.   1 JOHN 4:9-10

God's acceptance is based not on what a person does
but on faith in Jesus Christ. Even the most saintly human being is found lacking in comparison with God's
holiness. Nothing you do could ever compensate for the
sins that have separated you from God, who is perfect.
Fortunately, God's forgiveness flows from his love for
you, which is why he gave his Son, Jesus, to die before
you were even born or had committed your first sin.
God's acceptance has been waiting for you your whole
life. When you receive his forgiveness, he welcomes
you into his presence. What a wonderful moment it is

when you realize how fully God accepts you and are freed from the burden of trying to earn God's love.

DIVINE PROMISE

NOTHING . . . WILL EVER BE ABLE TO SEPARATE US FROM THE LOVE OF GOD THAT IS REVEALED IN CHRIST JESUS OUR LORD.   *Romans 8:39*

Addiction

MY QUESTION *for* GOD

How can God break the power of addiction in my life?

A MOMENT *with* GOD

You say, "I am allowed to do anything"—but not everything is good for you. And even though "I am allowed to do anything," I must not become a slave to anything.   1 CORINTHIANS 6:12

Don't copy the behavior and customs of this world, but let God transform you into a new person by changing the way you think. Then you will learn to know God's will for you, which is good and pleasing and perfect.   ROMANS 12:2

You belong to God, my dear children. You have already won a victory . . . because the Spirit who lives in you is greater than the spirit who lives in the world.   1 JOHN 4:4

The Holy Spirit produces this kind of fruit in our
lives: love, joy, peace, patience, kindness, goodness,
faithfulness, gentleness, and self-control.

GALATIANS 5:22-23

*W*ho in his or her right mind would volunteer to become a slave, held in bondage forever? Yet that's just
what addiction is: self-imposed slavery, selling yourself
to a lifetime of bondage to a habit or substance. While
you might typically think of addiction as a problem
related to drugs or alcohol, other addictions can be
just as destructive. You may become addicted to lazi-
ness, television, computer games, unhealthy food. The
list goes on and on. You can even be addicted to good
things such as exercise or even good food. We all have
our addictions, whether they are "minor" bad habits or
serious dependencies.

　　Sin is the greatest addiction. Like other substances
or habits, it often appears alluring and attractive, offering short-term pleasure. It's easy to justify giving
in "just this once" and thinking you have things under control. But soon you realize that what you are
giving in to has become a habit you can't stop, and it
now controls you. Sin, as with other addictions, often
comes from a loss of self-control. Ironically, the only
way to recover your self-control is to let God control
you. His control is always for your health, benefit, and
spiritual growth. God can break the power of addiction when you give him control of your life. That's
why it is imperative that you admit your addiction and
acknowledge its destructiveness. It is almost impos-

sible to overcome addiction by yourself. You need the consistent support of other people who love you, tell you the truth, and hold you accountable. But you must also hold yourself accountable to God's way of living as written in the Bible. As you stay close to God, he will change your heart and your desires. As you surrender to the Holy Spirit, God will replace addictive drives with life-affirming desires.

DIVINE PROMISE

YOU ARE NOT CONTROLLED BY YOUR SINFUL NATURE. YOU ARE CONTROLLED BY THE SPIRIT IF YOU HAVE THE SPIRIT OF GOD LIVING IN YOU. *Romans 8:9*

Adoption

MY QUESTION *for* GOD

How is adoption a picture of my relationship with God?

A MOMENT *with* GOD

To all who believed him and accepted him, he gave the right to become children of God. JOHN 1:12

When the right time came, God sent his Son, born of a woman, subject to the law. God sent him to buy freedom for us who were slaves to the law, so that he could adopt us as his very own children.

GALATIANS 4:4-5

Even before he made the world, God loved us and
chose us in Christ to be holy and without fault in his
eyes. God decided in advance to adopt us into his own
family by bringing us to himself through Jesus Christ.
This is what he wanted to do, and it gave him great
pleasure. So we praise God for the glorious grace he
has poured out on us who belong to his dear Son.

EPHESIANS 1:4-6

*Th*e process of adoption is a beautiful example of
God's love for you. Just as adoptive parents make a
choice to give a child a new life, Jesus chose to give
you a new life you couldn't otherwise achieve. People
who adopt children decide to lovingly teach and nurture them and give them rights and privileges of being
a member of the family. As a child of God, you are
privileged to receive all his blessings, both in this life
and the next.

DIVINE PROMISE

I WILL BE YOUR FATHER, AND YOU WILL
BE MY SONS AND DAUGHTERS, SAYS THE
LORD ALMIGHTY. *2 Corinthians 6:18*

Adversity

MY QUESTIONS *for* GOD

Is God listening when I cry to him in times of trouble?
Does it do any good to cry out to God?

A MOMENT *with* GOD

In my distress I cried out to the LORD; yes, I prayed
to my God for help. He heard me from his sanctuary;
my cry to him reached his ears.   PSALM 18:6

Jesus said, "Come to me, all of you who are weary
and carry heavy burdens, and I will give you rest."
                                         MATTHEW 11:28

Give all your worries and cares to God, for he cares
about you.   1 PETER 5:7

When troubles come your way, consider it an
opportunity for great joy. For you know that when
your faith is tested, your endurance has a chance
to grow.   JAMES 1:2-3

The Bible doesn't speculate about whether or not
trouble will come. It warns that trouble *will* come.
Your troubles don't mean that God has turned his back
on you or shut his ears to your prayers. God has both a
listening ear and a caring heart, and his Word assures
you that nothing can ever separate you from his love.
Adversity will come, but it brings with it opportunities
to strengthen your faith in God. If there were no troubles, you'd have no need for faith. You may often feel

that your need is impossible to meet, that you're too weak to go on, or that it's too late for solutions. Yet these are the times when God's power can be most evident in your life. Wait for the moment of God's rescue, and you will experience his presence in new and life-changing ways.

DIVINE PROMISE

CALL ON ME WHEN YOU ARE IN TROUBLE,
AND I WILL RESCUE YOU, AND YOU WILL GIVE
ME GLORY.   *Psalm 50:15*

Advice

MY QUESTIONS *for* GOD

I'm an intelligent person. Do I really need advice from others? Why?

A MOMENT *with* GOD

The instruction of the wise is like a life-giving fountain; those who accept it avoid the snares of death.   PROVERBS 13:14

Wise words are like deep waters; wisdom flows from the wise like a bubbling brook.   PROVERBS 18:4

Fools think their own way is right, but the wise listen to others.   PROVERBS 12:15

$\mathcal{G}$ood advice is not merely helpful; it also brings relief and comfort when it comes to you at just the right moment. God can use a conversation with a friend or even the advice of a trained counselor to bring about a turning point in your life. He often allows the words of others to reach us at the moment we are most ready to receive them. No one is wise enough to anticipate all the possibilities of a situation or to grasp all the issues related to a problem. Refusing to listen to others is a sign that you're not ready for change or spiritual growth. The right counsel can make the difference between success and failure, joy and sorrow, prosperity and poverty, victory and defeat. When you let go of your pride, you open yourself to receiving godly advice. At the critical moment, when you're most ready to hear it, God's wisdom will penetrate your heart.

DIVINE PROMISE

TRUE WISDOM AND POWER ARE FOUND
IN GOD; COUNSEL AND UNDERSTANDING
ARE HIS.   *Job 12:13*

Affirmation

MY QUESTION *for* GOD

How do I know that God truly values my life? How does he affirm me?

A MOMENT *with* GOD

God created human beings in his own image. In the image of God he created them; male and female he created them.   GENESIS 1:27

Long ago the LORD said to Israel: "I have loved you, my people, with an everlasting love. With unfailing love I have drawn you to myself."   JEREMIAH 31:3

God loved the world so much that he gave his one and only Son, so that everyone who believes in him will not perish but have eternal life. God sent his Son into the world not to judge the world, but to save the world through him.   JOHN 3:16-17

You can find affirmation in knowing that God chose to create you in his image and longs to have a relationship with you. God draws you to himself, even to the point of sacrificing his own Son to die for you so that you could be made perfect. Your life is the story of how God pursues you, rescues you from your sin, and restores you so that you can become the person you were created to be. Read God's words to you throughout the Bible, and think about all he has done to show you how much you matter to him. As you realize how fully God affirms your value, his love breaks through the messages the world sends about what you ought to be and instead encourages you to be what God wants you to be.

DIVINE PROMISE

WE KNOW WHAT REAL LOVE IS BECAUSE JESUS
GAVE UP HIS LIFE FOR US.   *1 John 3:16*

Agreement

MY QUESTION *for* GOD

*How can I find agreement with others without compromising
my convictions?*

A MOMENT *with* GOD

Daniel was determined not to defile himself by
eating the food. . . . He asked . . . permission not
to eat these unacceptable foods. . . . "Please test
us for ten days on a diet of vegetables and water,"
Daniel said. . . . The attendant agreed to Daniel's
suggestion. . . . At the end of the ten days, Daniel
. . . looked healthier and better nourished than the
young men who had been eating the food assigned
by the king.   DANIEL 1:8, 12-15

*W*hen you are trying to reach an agreement with
someone else, there is a time to compromise and a time
to hold firm. When the forces of evil want their way,
you cannot budge. To compromise God's truth, God's
ways, or God's Word is to negotiate with what is unholy. The test of acceptable compromise is simple: Can
two parties reach a mutually satisfactory agreement
without either party sacrificing his or her morals? To

give up godliness for anything is a bad bargain. Work for harmony and agreement wherever possible, and where that is not possible, pray that God would break through the stalemate to make his will clear.

DIVINE PROMISE

BE ON GUARD. STAND FIRM IN THE FAITH. BE COURAGEOUS. BE STRONG.   *1 Corinthians 16:13*

Amazement

MY QUESTION *for* GOD

How can I capture or recapture a sense of amazement about God?

A MOMENT *with* GOD

I have heard all about you, LORD. I am filled with awe by your amazing works.   HABAKKUK 3:2

You are the God of great wonders! You demonstrate your awesome power among the nations.   PSALM 77:14

The heavens proclaim the glory of God. The skies display his craftsmanship. Day after day they continue to speak; night after night they make him known.

PSALM 19:1-2

$\mathscr{P}$ay attention—to the stories of others and to the world around you. God is doing amazing work everywhere. Don't forget the quiet miracles that take place each day: the birth of a baby, a beautiful sunset, close friends, a feeling of joy in the midst of overwhelming circumstances. Being in awe of God over these "small" miracles prepares your heart to experience even more amazing things from God. Listen to how God has amazed others, and add those amazing events to your own list. The more you look for evidence of God's work, the more amazed you will be.

DIVINE PROMISE

HE HAS GIVEN ME A NEW SONG TO SING, A HYMN OF PRAISE TO OUR GOD. MANY WILL SEE WHAT HE HAS DONE AND BE AMAZED. THEY WILL PUT THEIR TRUST IN THE LORD.   *Psalm 40:3*

$\mathscr{A}mbition$

MY QUESTION *for* GOD

When is ambition dangerous?

A MOMENT *with* GOD

The devil took [Jesus] to the peak of a very high mountain and showed him all the kingdoms of the world and their glory. "I will give it all to you," he said, "if you will kneel down and worship me." "Get out of here, Satan," Jesus told him. "For the

Scriptures say, 'You must worship the LORD your
God and serve only him.'"   MATTHEW 4:8-10

There's a difference between wanting to be a part
of God's great work and wanting to achieve personal
greatness through doing God's work. It's the difference
between desiring to serve God and trying to use God
to serve you. It is instructive and even frightening that
Satan, the Deceiver, believed he could tempt Jesus by
appealing to his sense of ambition. How many have sold
their souls to the devil in an attempt to gain worldly
glory? Selfish ambition, left unchecked, becomes the
hook Satan uses to reel us in. If Jesus had been motivated by selfish ambition rather than by the will and
Word of God, he would have been vulnerable to the
temptation to possess the kingdoms and splendor of the
world. If you had to make a list of your five primary
ambitions, what would they be? If someone else were
asked to list your five main ambitions would the two
lists match? Ambition can become destructive if Satan
uses it to lure you away from God. You can test your
ambitions by asking if what you want to do will bring
you closer to God or move you further away from him.
If you're not sure, then that ambition is likely leading
you away from him. Ambition can fool you into striving
to gain all you desire in this world at the cost of all God
desires for you both here and in heaven.

DIVINE PROMISE

WHEN YOU FOLLOW THE DESIRES OF YOUR
SINFUL NATURE, THE RESULTS ARE VERY CLEAR:
. . . HOSTILITY, QUARRELING, JEALOUSY,
OUTBURSTS OF ANGER, SELFISH AMBITION,
DISSENSION, DIVISION, ENVY . . . AND OTHER
SINS LIKE THESE. . . . BUT THE HOLY SPIRIT
PRODUCES THIS KIND OF FRUIT IN OUR
LIVES: LOVE, JOY, PEACE, PATIENCE, KINDNESS,
GOODNESS, FAITHFULNESS. *Galatians 5:19-22*

Angels

MY QUESTIONS *for* GOD

Are angels real? Will I be an angel in heaven?

A MOMENT *with* GOD

Praise him, all his angels! Praise him, all the armies
of heaven. . . . Let every created thing give praise to
the LORD, for he issued his command, and they came
into being. PSALM 148:2, 5

Angels are only servants—spirits sent to care for
people who will inherit salvation. HEBREWS 1:14

Don't you realize that someday we believers will
judge the world? . . . Don't you realize that we will
judge angels? 1 CORINTHIANS 6:2-3

Angels, like humans, are real beings created by God.
Just as God creates each person as a unique individual,

he created angels as unique beings. For example, some angels in the Bible, like Michael and Gabriel, are mentioned by name and were given specific tasks, such as protecting people or delivering messages from God. God uses his angels to counsel, guide, protect, minister to, rescue, fight for, and care for his people. Whether he assigns one angel to a specific individual or uses his host of angels is his choice and your blessing. Thank God for the unseen ways in which angels may have touched you. Chances are that angels have played a greater role in your life than you realize.

DIVINE PROMISE

HE WILL ORDER HIS ANGELS TO PROTECT YOU
WHEREVER YOU GO.   *Psalm 91:11*

Anger

MY QUESTION *for* GOD

Why do I most often get angry?

A MOMENT *with* GOD

The LORD accepted Abel and his gift, but he did not accept Cain and his gift. This made Cain very angry, and he looked dejected.   GENESIS 4:4-5

"You have made me look like a fool!" Balaam shouted. "If I had a sword with me, I would kill you!"

NUMBERS 22:29

"Didn't I tell you?" the king of Israel exclaimed. . . .
"He never prophesies anything but trouble for me.
. . . Put this man in prison, and feed him nothing
but bread and water until I return safely from the
battle!"   1 KINGS 22:18, 27

"Get out of the sanctuary, for you have sinned." . . .
Uzziah, who was holding an incense burner, became
furious. But as he was standing there raging at the
priests before the incense altar in the LORD's Temple,
leprosy suddenly broke out on his forehead.

                                               2 CHRONICLES 26:18-19

All the king's officials would bow down before
Haman to show him respect whenever he passed
by, for so the king had commanded. But Mordecai
refused to bow down or show him respect. . . . When
Haman saw that Mordecai would not bow down or
show him respect, he was filled with rage.

                                                        ESTHER 3:2, 5

The earnest prayer of a righteous person has great
power and produces wonderful results.   JAMES 5:16

Anger is often a reaction to having your pride hurt.
When you are confronted, rejected, ignored, or don't
get your own way, anger is a defense mechanism used
to protect your ego. It is common to feel angry when
someone has confronted you about your own sinful actions, because you don't want others to think you have
done something wrong. Train yourself to examine your
heart whenever you become angry. Ask yourself, Who

is really offended in this situation? Is this about God's honor or my pride? Prayer is a mighty weapon in overcoming anger. It is hard to stay angry at someone when you are praying for that person.

DIVINE PROMISE

A GENTLE ANSWER DEFLECTS ANGER, BUT
HARSH WORDS MAKE TEMPERS FLARE.

Proverbs 15:1

Anticipation

MY QUESTIONS *for* GOD

Why should I anticipate eternal life? What do I have to look forward to there?

A MOMENT *with* GOD

Against its will, all creation was subjected to God's curse. But with eager hope, the creation looks forward to the day when it will join God's children in glorious freedom from death and decay. For we know that all creation has been groaning as in the pains of childbirth right up to the present time. And we believers also groan, even though we have the Holy Spirit within us as a foretaste of future glory, for we long for our bodies to be released from sin and suffering. We, too, wait with eager hope for the day when God will give us our full rights as his

adopted children, including the new bodies he has
promised us.   ROMANS 8:20-23

Dear brothers and sisters, be patient as you wait
for the Lord's return. Consider the farmers who
patiently wait for the rains in the fall and in the
spring. They eagerly look for the valuable harvest to
ripen. You, too, must be patient. Take courage, for
the coming of the Lord is near.   JAMES 5:7-8

When you finally take your long-awaited vacation,
you may have anticipated it for weeks or months leading
up to the time you leave. You've planned and prepared,
but you don't know exactly how it will go once you're
there. You do know enough to look forward to your
time of much needed rest and recreation with pleasure.
This is similar to the hope you should have for heaven.
God reveals just enough about your eternal home to
give you something to anticipate with joy and to encourage you to obey. Just as you still have to go to work
to earn your vacation in this life, you will still have
some struggles to work through before you can enter
heaven. Everyone dreams of moments of joy and times
of real rest. God has promised you these things! Are
you eager to see what he has planned for you?

DIVINE PROMISE

WE LIVE WITH GREAT EXPECTATION, AND
WE HAVE A PRICELESS INHERITANCE—AN
INHERITANCE THAT IS KEPT IN HEAVEN

FOR YOU, PURE AND UNDEFILED, BEYOND
THE REACH OF CHANGE AND DECAY. AND
THROUGH YOUR FAITH, GOD IS PROTECTING
YOU BY HIS POWER UNTIL YOU RECEIVE THIS
SALVATION, WHICH IS READY TO BE REVEALED
ON THE LAST DAY FOR ALL TO SEE. SO BE TRULY
GLAD. THERE IS WONDERFUL JOY AHEAD, EVEN
THOUGH YOU HAVE TO ENDURE MANY TRIALS
FOR A LITTLE WHILE.   *1 Peter 1:3-6*

Apology

MY QUESTION *for* GOD

Why is it so important to apologize to someone I've wronged?

A MOMENT *with* GOD

The high and lofty one who lives in eternity, the
Holy One, says this: "I live in the high and holy place
with those whose spirits are contrite and humble.
I restore the crushed spirit of the humble and revive
the courage of those with repentant hearts.   ISAIAH 57:15

Confess your sins to each other and pray for each
other so that you may be healed.   JAMES 5:16

Fools make fun of guilt, but the godly acknowledge it
and seek reconciliation.   PROVERBS 14:9

A true apology takes genuine humility. It requires
that you realize your fault and admit it to another. It's
often tempting to pretend the offense never happened,

to try to cover it up, or to avoid the other person. These are signs that your heart is proud and averse to taking responsibility for your actions. Refusing to apologize can have devastating consequences in your life: sour relationships, bitterness, isolation, rage, guilt. But through an apology you can experience reconciliation, forgiveness, healing, and courage. These are the blessings that come with a tender conscience and a humble heart. Lasting change can begin only in a humble heart. At the moment you admit your fault and ask forgiveness, you will begin to experience God's healing in your heart and your relationships. Is it time for you to apologize to God and others?

DIVINE PROMISE

PEOPLE WHO CONCEAL THEIR SINS WILL NOT PROSPER, BUT IF THEY CONFESS AND TURN FROM THEM, THEY WILL RECEIVE MERCY.

Proverbs 28:13

Appearance

MY QUESTION *for* GOD

How much does appearance matter?

A MOMENT *with* GOD

Don't be concerned about the outward beauty of fancy hairstyles, expensive jewelry, or beautiful clothes. You should clothe yourselves instead with the beauty that comes from within, the unfading beauty of a gentle and quiet spirit, which is so precious to God.   1 PETER 3:3-4

Charm is deceptive, and beauty does not last; but a woman who fears the LORD will be greatly praised.

PROVERBS 31:30

If you listen to the word and don't obey, it is like glancing at your face in a mirror. You see yourself, walk away, and forget what you look like.   JAMES 1:23-24

*A*ppearance does matter; just make sure you're looking at the right things. Your body, face, and clothes reflect only your outward shell, which is in a constant process of aging and decay. Your soul and character reflect your inner being, which is ageless and eternal and shows who you really are. In other words, the condition of your body does not reveal the condition of your heart. There's nothing wrong with paying attention to your physical appearance, but not to the neglect of your spiritual appearance. It's easy for us to get distracted and focus on our own appearance or the appearance of others (looking for those who seem most impressive to us). But what an impact we can have on others when they miss what's on our outside because they can't take their eyes off what's on the inside—the light of God's love and truth shining through us. Walking with God causes you to reflect his beauty.

DIVINE PROMISE

PEOPLE JUDGE BY OUTWARD APPEARANCE, BUT THE LORD LOOKS AT THE HEART.   *1 Samuel 16:7*

Appreciation

MY QUESTION *for* GOD

Why is it important to appreciate "the little things in life"?

A MOMENT *with* GOD

It is good to give thanks to the LORD, to sing praises to the Most High. It is good to proclaim your unfailing love in the morning, your faithfulness in the evening.   PSALM 92:1-2

Every time I think of you, I give thanks to my God. Whenever I pray, I make my requests for all of you with joy.   PHILIPPIANS 1:3-4

Be thankful in all circumstances, for this is God's will for you who belong to Christ Jesus.

          1 THESSALONIANS 5:18

*O*ne of the best ways to experience God is to notice and appreciate the little things around you. Turning your focus outward helps you to see many things to be thankful for. Rather than say "I wish," try saying, "I'm thankful." Cultivate an appreciative heart by giving thanks regularly, consistently, and spontaneously.

This kind of attitude helps to keep life's disappointments from blinding you to what God is doing in the
here and now. Every moment is an opportunity to see
God's provision and presence.

DIVINE PROMISE

GIVE THANKS TO THE LORD, FOR HE IS GOOD!
HIS FAITHFUL LOVE ENDURES FOREVER.
1 Chronicles 16:34

Armor of God

MY QUESTION *for* GOD

*How do I use the armor of God to stay strong during the
battles of life?*

A MOMENT *with* GOD

Be strong in the Lord and in his mighty power. Put
on all of God's armor so that you will be able to
stand firm against all strategies of the devil. For we
are not fighting against flesh-and-blood enemies,
but against evil rulers and authorities of the unseen
world, against mighty powers in this dark world, and
against evil spirits in the heavenly places. Therefore,
put on every piece of God's armor so you will be able
to resist the enemy in the time of evil. Then after
the battle you will still be standing firm. Stand your
ground, putting on the belt of truth and the body
armor of God's righteousness. For shoes, put on the

peace that comes from the Good News so that you will be fully prepared. In addition to all of these, hold up the shield of faith to stop the fiery arrows of the devil. Put on salvation as your helmet, and take the sword of the Spirit, which is the word of God.

EPHESIANS 6:10-17

*A*lthough armor may feel heavy and cumbersome, it is effective in keeping you safe against attack only when it is worn! Wearing God's armor will help you win the battles in life brought on by the attacks of Satan and those who oppose God. You will be fully prepared when you have protected your body with the armor of righteousness, strapped on the belt of truth, walked in peace, shielded yourself with faith, protected your mind with salvation, and prepared to pierce evil with the sword of God's Word.

DIVINE PROMISE

THIS IS WHAT THE LORD SAYS: DO NOT BE AFRAID! DON'T BE DISCOURAGED BY THIS MIGHTY ARMY, FOR THE BATTLE IS NOT YOURS, BUT GOD'S. *2 Chronicles 20:15*

Assurance

Where can I find assurance amid the uncertainties of life?
Can I be sure of anything?

A MOMENT *with* GOD

Blessed are those who trust in the LORD and have
made the LORD their hope and confidence. They
are like trees planted along a riverbank, with roots
that reach deep into the water. Such trees are not
bothered by the heat or worried by long months of
drought. Their leaves stay green, and they never stop
producing fruit.   JEREMIAH 17:7-8

It is better to take refuge in the LORD than to trust
in people.   PSALM 118:8

Oh, the joys of those who trust the LORD, who
have no confidence in the proud or in those who
worship idols.   PSALM 40:4

One thing you can always be certain of is God's love
for you. When you go through hard times, it doesn't
mean that God has abandoned you. Rather, hard times
allow God to reveal his infinite love and care for you.
Assurance from other relationships is good at times,
but God is the only one in whom you can trust completely without fear of disappointment. You can be
assured that what he says is true and what he does is
reliable. The world is filled with uncertainty, so why

search for assurance in it? Assurance in this life comes from experiencing God's love for you, which gives you security for today and for eternity.

DIVINE PROMISE

LISTEN TO THE LORD WHO CREATED YOU. . . . THE ONE WHO FORMED YOU SAYS, "DO NOT BE AFRAID, FOR I HAVE RANSOMED YOU. I HAVE CALLED YOU BY NAME; YOU ARE MINE. WHEN YOU GO THROUGH DEEP WATERS, I WILL BE WITH YOU. WHEN YOU GO THROUGH RIVERS OF DIFFICULTY, YOU WILL NOT DROWN. WHEN YOU WALK THROUGH THE FIRE OF OPPRESSION, YOU WILL NOT BE BURNED UP; THE FLAMES WILL NOT CONSUME YOU. FOR I AM THE LORD, YOUR GOD, THE HOLY ONE OF ISRAEL, YOUR SAVIOR." *Isaiah 43:1-3*

Attitude

MY QUESTION *for* GOD

Is attitude really everything?

A MOMENT *with* GOD

You must have the same attitude that Christ Jesus had. Though he was God, he did not think of equality with God as something to cling to. Instead, he gave up his divine privileges; he took the humble position of a slave and was born as a human being. When he appeared in human form, he humbled himself in

obedience to God and died a criminal's death on
a cross.   PHILIPPIANS 2:5-8

Always be full of joy in the Lord. I say it again—
rejoice! . . . Don't worry about anything; instead,
pray about everything. Tell God what you need, and
thank him for all he has done.   PHILIPPIANS 4:4-6

Always be joyful. Never stop praying. Be thankful in
all circumstances, for this is God's will for you who
belong to Christ Jesus.   1 THESSALONIANS 5:16-18

*A*ttitude plays a huge role in how you view life. What
you think about something determines whether you
will do anything about it. Your attitudes certainly affect your actions. But the opposite is also true. Your
actions can affect your attitudes. In fact, one of the
best ways to change your attitude is to start with the
action that points to the right attitude. When your actions focus on obeying and loving an eternal God, you
become infused with a sense of eternal purpose rather
than feelings of religious obligation. Don't be resent-
ful if you haven't experienced God. Rather, seek out
the actions that will lead you to him! The bottom line
is this: Life is more about how you react to your circumstances than about what actually happens to you.
That's why the Bible doesn't *suggest* being joyful or generous—it commands it!

DIVINE PROMISE

THE KINGDOM OF GOD IS NOT A MATTER OF
WHAT WE EAT OR DRINK, BUT OF LIVING A LIFE
OF GOODNESS AND PEACE AND JOY IN THE
HOLY SPIRIT. IF YOU SERVE CHRIST WITH THIS
ATTITUDE, YOU WILL PLEASE GOD.   *Romans 14:17-18*

Availability

MY QUESTION *for* GOD

What does it mean to be available to God?

A MOMENT *with* GOD

If any of you wants to be my follower, you must turn
from your selfish ways, take up your cross, and follow
me. If you try to hang on to your life, you will lose
it. But if you give up your life for my sake and for the
sake of the Good News, you will save it.   MARK 8:34-35

As soon as they landed, they left everything and
followed Jesus.   LUKE 5:11

My sheep listen to my voice; I know them, and they
follow me.   JOHN 10:27

To be available to God means more than just acknowledging his existence. It means reorienting your life so
that no matter what you do, you do it as service to
him. Availability means that you have an eagerness to
go where he calls you and serve where he shows you.

It is simply a matter of following God with a willing heart. He will bless you, not because of your ability but because of your availability.

DIVINE PROMISE

BE STRONG AND COURAGEOUS, AND DO THE WORK. DON'T BE AFRAID OR DISCOURAGED, FOR THE LORD GOD, MY GOD, IS WITH YOU. HE WILL NOT FAIL YOU OR FORSAKE YOU.

1 Chronicles 28:20

Awesomeness

MY QUESTIONS *for* GOD

What happens in me when I recognize the awesomeness of God? Why do I need to see it?

A MOMENT *with* GOD

Who is like you among the gods, O LORD—glorious in holiness, awesome in splendor, performing great wonders?   EXODUS 15:11

Who can comprehend the power of your anger? Your wrath is as awesome as the fear you deserve.

PSALM 90:11

Everyone was gripped with great wonder and awe, and they praised God, exclaiming, "We have seen amazing things today!"   LUKE 5:26

$\mathcal{F}$ear of God is different from a fear of other power-ful things. You hide from the power of a severe storm or run from the power of a large wave crashing on the shore. But the awesomeness of God's power is captivat-ing. The more you see God's awesomeness at work in your life and the world around you, the more you will desire to be near him and experience his empowering Spirit. Recognizing God's awesomeness puts you in the middle of his glory and helps you experience both God's presence and his unconditional love.

DIVINE PROMISE

I HAVE HEARD ALL ABOUT YOU, LORD. I AM
FILLED WITH AWE BY YOUR AMAZING WORKS.
IN THIS TIME OF OUR DEEP NEED, HELP US
AGAIN AS YOU DID IN YEARS GONE BY. AND IN
YOUR ANGER, REMEMBER YOUR MERCY.
Habakkuk 3:2

$\mathcal{B}$alance

MY QUESTION *for* GOD

*With all my responsibilities at work and at home, how do
I achieve balance?*

A MOMENT *with* GOD

I run with purpose in every step. I am not just
shadowboxing. I discipline my body like an athlete,
training it to do what it should.   1 CORINTHIANS 9:26-27

For everything there is a season, a time for every
activity under heaven.   ECCLESIASTES 3:1

Just as our bodies have many parts and each part has
a special function, so it is with Christ's body. We are
many parts of one body, and we all belong to each
other. In his grace, God has given us different gifts
for doing certain things well.   ROMANS 12:4-6

I brought glory to you here on earth by completing
the work you gave me to do. Now, Father, bring me
into the glory we shared before the world began.

                                               JOHN 17:4-5

*L*iving a balanced life means you honor God, others,
and yourself with the way you use your gifts and spend
your time and resources. It's easy to get out of balance
by overemphasizing one aspect of your responsibilities
at the cost of other areas. God assures you that there is
a time for everything as well as time for everything he
calls us to do. Jesus, with all his potential and all the
needs around him, left much undone, yet he accomplished everything God had given him to do. You will
find true peace and contentment when you realize that
you don't have to do everything, only those things God
created you to do. Then you will find balance, knowing
that in God's eyes you are doing all you need to.

DIVINE CHALLENGE
YOU ARE A SLAVE TO WHATEVER
CONTROLS YOU.   *2 Peter 2:19*

Beauty

MY QUESTION *for* GOD

How can I learn to see God in the beauty around me?

A MOMENT *with* GOD

The sun has one kind of glory, while the moon and stars each have another kind. And even the stars differ from each other in their glory.   1 CORINTHIANS 15:41

Honor and majesty surround him; strength and beauty fill his sanctuary.   PSALM 96:6

Look at the lilies and how they grow. They don't work or make their clothing, yet Solomon in all his glory was not dressed as beautifully as they are.

LUKE 12:27

*L*earning to find beauty in life is one of the best ways to prepare your heart and mind for moments with God. The majesty of the mountains, the sound of falling rain, the smell of burning leaves, the touch of a loved one, the taste of your favorite meal—God's beauty is all around you, bombarding every one of your senses. When you learn to recognize and appreciate God's beauty, you will often find yourself experiencing God in his creations.

DIVINE PROMISE

GOD HAS MADE EVERYTHING BEAUTIFUL FOR
ITS OWN TIME. HE HAS PLANTED ETERNITY
IN THE HUMAN HEART, BUT EVEN SO, PEOPLE
CANNOT SEE THE WHOLE SCOPE OF GOD'S
WORK FROM BEGINNING TO END.

Ecclesiastes 3:11

Belonging

MY QUESTION *for* GOD

What are the privileges of belonging to God?

A MOMENT *with* GOD

Those who die in the LORD will live; their bodies
will rise again!   ISAIAH 26:19

Now that you belong to Christ, you are the true
children of Abraham. You are his heirs, and God's
promise to Abraham belongs to you.   GALATIANS 3:29

All praise to God, the Father of our Lord Jesus
Christ, who has blessed us with every spiritual
blessing in the heavenly realms because we are
united with Christ.   EPHESIANS 1:3

Belonging to God brings so many privileges. It means
you are no longer enslaved to sin; you can overcome it.
Belonging to God means you can be certain that you will
rise from the dead, live eternally with God, and receive

all that God has promised his people in the Bible. On earth you can experience blessings like peace of heart, comfort, Christian friendships, and fulfillment, knowing you are doing what God has created you to do. The privileges of belonging to God are countless, and the more you give yourself to him, the more you will discover and experience of these privileges.

Divine Promise

THE ETERNAL GOD IS YOUR REFUGE, AND HIS EVERLASTING ARMS ARE UNDER YOU.

Deuteronomy 33:27

Bible

My Question *for* God

What can I experience when reading the Bible?

A Moment *with* God

The instructions of the LORD are perfect, reviving the soul. The decrees of the LORD are trustworthy, making wise the simple. The commandments of the LORD are right, bringing joy to the heart. The commands of the LORD are clear, giving insight for living.   PSALM 19:7-8

Your promise revives me; it comforts me in all my troubles.   PSALM 119:50

All Scripture is inspired by God and is useful to teach us what is true and to make us realize what is wrong in our lives. It corrects us when we are wrong and teaches us to do what is right. God uses it to prepare and equip his people to do every good work.

2 TIMOTHY 3:16-17

*B*ecause the Bible is the Word of God, it is the only document that is "living." In other words, it is relevant for all people in all places in any time period. Because the Bible is a living document through which God speaks, daily reading is important. It's easy to become distracted and lose touch with God. Reading his Word every day keeps you in the presence of the One who created you for a purpose, knows you best, and can guide you along the best pathway for your life. If you open your heart to the words recorded in this book, you will begin to experience comfort, joy, insight, wisdom, knowledge, and the keys to living.

DIVINE PROMISE

THE LAWS OF THE LORD ARE TRUE; EACH ONE IS FAIR. THEY ARE MORE DESIRABLE THAN GOLD, EVEN THE FINEST GOLD. THEY ARE SWEETER THAN HONEY, EVEN HONEY DRIPPING FROM THE COMB. *Psalm 19:9-10*

Blessings

MY QUESTION *for* GOD

How can I experience God's blessings?

A MOMENT *with* GOD

You will experience all these blessings if you obey the
LORD your God.   DEUTERONOMY 28:2

How joyful are those who fear the LORD—all who
follow his ways! . . . That is the LORD's blessing for
those who fear him.   PSALM 128:1, 4

All must give as they are able, according to the
blessings given to them by the LORD your God.
                              DEUTERONOMY 16:17

Give as freely as you have received!   MATTHEW 10:8

God's love is like an ocean, with wave after wave of
his blessings flowing over you. Like the constant move-
ment of the water, God's blessings are also constant to
those who love him and share his blessings with others.
In the Bible, God has promised those who love him rich
blessings, including his presence, his grace, his comfort, his provision, and his peace. But God doesn't want
to be loved only for his blessings. The sign of true love
for God is obedience—helping others and serving the
Lord. If you want God to bless you just so you can live
a comfortable life, then you misunderstand why God
blesses his people. God will bless you when you want

him to pour his blessings through you in order to bless
others. God's blessings work through his people.

DIVINE PROMISE

THE LORD GOD IS OUR SUN AND OUR SHIELD.
HE GIVES US GRACE AND GLORY. THE LORD
WILL WITHHOLD NO GOOD THING FROM
THOSE WHO DO WHAT IS RIGHT. *Psalm 84:11*

Boredom

MY QUESTION *for* GOD

How can I deal with boredom?

A MOMENT *with* GOD

Imitate God, therefore, in everything you do. . . .
Live a life filled with love, following the example
of Christ.   EPHESIANS 5:1-2

Don't look out only for your own interests, but take
an interest in others, too.   PHILIPPIANS 2:4

Merriam-Webster's Collegiate Dictionary defines *boredom* as "the state of being weary and restless through
lack of interest." You might become bored from doing the same thing over and over, or from doing work
with no apparent purpose, or from doing nothing for
too long. Many people with hectic schedules say, "I'd

love to be bored for a while." But there's a difference between boredom and rest. We all need rest; but we don't need boredom. Boredom is dangerous because it can signify a lack of purpose and a lack of passion for anything meaningful. The antidote to boredom is finding something purposeful and significant to do. God has a purpose for you. Discovering that purpose is a divine moment and from that time on you will never be bored. Start by volunteering to help in a ministry in your local church. Find a hobby that helps you develop a skill (music, crafts, etc.). Then you will have something to look forward to each day. A fire will ignite in your heart, and people will be attracted to your enthusiasm and passion for living.

DIVINE PROMISE

LET'S NOT GET TIRED OF DOING WHAT IS GOOD. AT JUST THE RIGHT TIME WE WILL REAP A HARVEST OF BLESSING IF WE DON'T GIVE UP.

Galatians 6:9

Brokenness

MY QUESTION *for* GOD

My heart is breaking. I'm overwhelmed, and my life is a mess. Is there any hope?

A MOMENT *with* GOD

The sacrifice you desire is a broken spirit. You will
not reject a broken and repentant heart, O God.

PSALM 51:17

Have mercy on me, O God, because of your unfailing
love. Because of your great compassion, blot out
the stain of my sins. Wash me clean from my guilt.
Purify me from my sin. For I recognize my rebellion;
it haunts me day and night. Against you, and you
alone, have I sinned; I have done what is evil in your
sight. You will be proved right in what you say, and
your judgment against me is just.   PSALM 51:1-4

*B*rokenness itself can be a divine moment with God.
Brokenness comes most often through circumstances
that overwhelm you or through sin that reduces you to
the point where you realize that the only way out of
your mess is by God's help. It is a feeling of hitting bottom and realizing your complete dependence on God.
Brokenness also comes as you grow in the awareness
of God's holiness in contrast to your own sinfulness.
It signifies the breaking point of your pride and self-
sufficiency and becomes a turning point in your life.
It is the moment when you release control of your life
into God's loving hands. When you are brokenhearted
about sin in your life, God promises to draw close to
you, heal your self-inflicted wounds, and restore you
to himself.

DIVINE PROMISE

THE LORD IS CLOSE TO THE BROKENHEARTED;
HE RESCUES THOSE WHOSE SPIRITS
ARE CRUSHED.   *Psalm 34:18*

Building Others Up

MY QUESTION *for* GOD

Why should I work to build others up?

A MOMENT *with* GOD

We should help others do what is right and build
them up in the Lord.   ROMANS 15:2

Let us think of ways to motivate one another to acts
of love and good works.   HEBREWS 10:24

All of you should be of one mind. Sympathize with
each other. Love each other as brothers and sisters.
Be tenderhearted, and keep a humble attitude.

1 PETER 3:8

God designed the church so that everyone who believes in him can find encouragement and belonging in
a community. God commands you to build others up
as a means of strengthening the church and the faith of
others. He also wants you pay attention to others outside the church community and to care for their needs
as well. In this way, you will be strengthening the faith
of other believers, but you can also help others who

don't believe to experience God's love. Perhaps your kind smile, encouraging words, or simple help, will be the divine moment that allows others to experience the reality and depths of God's love for them. Perhaps there was a time in your life when you felt God's rich love flowing through another. When you're open to serving others, you can be the source of someone else's breakthrough with God.

DIVINE PROMISE

DEAR BROTHERS AND SISTERS . . . BE JOYFUL.
GROW TO MATURITY. ENCOURAGE EACH
OTHER. LIVE IN HARMONY AND PEACE.
THEN THE GOD OF LOVE AND PEACE WILL
BE WITH YOU.   *2 Corinthians 13:11*

Burnout

MY QUESTION *for* GOD

I'm burning the candle at both ends. How do I find extra strength when it seems I have little left?

A MOMENT *with* GOD

When David and his men were in the thick of battle, David became weak and exhausted.   2 SAMUEL 21:15

I am exhausted and completely crushed. My groans come from an anguished heart.   PSALM 38:8

Only in returning to me and resting in me will
you be saved. In quietness and confidence is your
strength.   ISAIAH 30:15

Come to me, all of you who are weary and carry
heavy burdens, and I will give you rest.   MATTHEW 11:28

He gives power to the weak and strength to the powerless. Even youths will become weak and tired, and
young men will fall in exhaustion. But those who trust
in the LORD will find new strength. They will soar
high on wings like eagles. They will run and not grow
weary. They will walk and not faint.   ISAIAH 40:29-31

*B*urnout is overwhelming exhaustion and inability
to push on brought about by too much stress. We all
experience times of burnout when we feel tapped out
emotionally, mentally, physically, and spiritually. In
our fast-paced world of "open all night" and "twenty-
four-hour service," it isn't surprising that we quickly
become exhausted. Because burnout is so draining
and paralyzing, we need to take care of our bodies and
minds by eating right, exercising, and getting enough
rest. Otherwise, we can't function effectively. One of
the best ways to reduce burnout is to take time out
to be close to God. Usually when we're burning the
candle at both ends, we are neglecting our time with
God. When we draw close to him, we can tap into his
power, strength, peace, protection, and love. Schedule
time to meditate on his Word and on a good book that
challenges you spiritually. As you focus on God's priorities, your own priorities will become clearer.

DIVINE PROMISE

THE LORD IS MY SHEPHERD; I HAVE ALL THAT I
NEED. HE LETS ME REST IN GREEN MEADOWS;
HE LEADS ME BESIDE PEACEFUL STREAMS.
HE RENEWS MY STRENGTH. HE GUIDES ME
ALONG RIGHT PATHS, BRINGING HONOR
TO HIS NAME.   *Psalm 23:1-3*

Busyness

MY QUESTION *for* GOD

How can busyness hinder my experience of God?

A MOMENT *with* GOD

We are merely moving shadows, and all our busy
rushing ends in nothing. We heap up wealth, not
knowing who will spend it.   PSALM 39:6

You have six days each week for your ordinary work,
but on the seventh day you must stop working, even
during the seasons of plowing and harvest. EXODUS 34:21

Be careful how you live. Don't live like fools,
but like those who are wise. Make the most of
every opportunity in these evil days. Don't act
thoughtlessly, but understand what the Lord wants
you to do.   EPHESIANS 5:15-17

Activity itself is not a virtue; in fact, it can actually be
a detriment to your spiritual life because it can quickly

lead you away from God. This is why God doesn't demand constant activity; he desires both productive activity and refreshing rest. Sometimes God pursues his
people. He may be trying to get your attention for a
moment with him. Enthusiastic service is important,
but it is just as important to take time to be still and
listen to him. Busyness in your life overcrowds your
mental resources, leaving no possibility for the quiet
moments with God in which he can guide and refresh
you. Even though he may be trying to break through to
you, you will never recognize it until you slow down
and allow time for him.

DIVINE PROMISE

TEACH US TO REALIZE THE BREVITY OF LIFE, SO
THAT WE MAY GROW IN WISDOM.   *Psalm 90:12*

Call of God

MY QUESTION *for* GOD

How do I know when God is calling me to do something?

A MOMENT *with* GOD

Let God transform you into a new person by
changing the way you think. Then you will learn to
know God's will for you, which is good and pleasing
and perfect.   ROMANS 12:2

A spiritual gift is given to each of us so we can help
each other.   1 CORINTHIANS 12:7

When the LORD saw Moses coming to take a closer
look, God called to him from the middle of the bush,
"Moses! Moses!" "Here I am!" Moses replied. . . .
Then the LORD told him, . . . "Go, for I am sending
you to Pharaoh. You must lead my people Israel out
of Egypt."   EXODUS 3:4, 7, 10

The LORD called out, "Samuel!" . . . And Samuel
replied, "Speak, your servant is listening."
                                                1 SAMUEL 3:4, 10

Your word is a lamp to guide my feet and a light for
my path.   PSALM 119:105

*T*he first step in knowing your calling is getting to
know God intimately through his Word. As God communicates to you through the Bible and as you pray, he
will show you what he wants you to do and where he
wants you to go. God always calls you in two different
ways: general and specific. God's general call is to obey
his Word, do what is right, and show genuine love for
others. But God also has a specific call for each person,
a special role he wants you to play, based on the unique
gifts he has given you. For most of us, that call will not
be as obvious as it was to Moses or Samuel in the verses
above. When God is ready to call you to a specific task,
he will keep interrupting your thoughts. Your heart
will long to do what God wants you to do; you will
know it is what you should do. Then opportunities to

serve will follow again and again. Seize the moment, and follow God's call. Don't let the window of opportunity close and miss all God has in store for you.

DIVINE CHALLENGE

YOU DIDN'T CHOOSE ME. I CHOSE YOU.
I APPOINTED YOU TO GO AND PRODUCE
LASTING FRUIT.   *John 15:16*

Care

MY QUESTION *for* GOD

I feel as if nobody else cares about me. Why would God care about me?

A MOMENT *with* GOD

You have been with me from birth; from my mother's womb you have cared for me. No wonder I am always praising you!   PSALM 71:6

I will be glad and rejoice in your unfailing love, for you have seen my troubles, and you care about the anguish of my soul.   PSALM 31:7

If God cares so wonderfully for wildflowers that are here today and thrown into the fire tomorrow, he will certainly care for you.   MATTHEW 6:30

Give all your worries and cares to God, for he cares about you.   1 PETER 5:7

God's care for you is deeply personal. His love for you began before you were born, continues throughout your life, and extends throughout eternity. He created you to have a relationship with him, and he gives you the opportunity to live with him forever. In addition, God's care for you is unique. Only he knows how to love you in ways that you will respond to and that will make you feel cared for. In fact, he urges you to bring your needs and worries to him because he cares so much about what happens to you. It is natural to feel lonely when others desert or abandon you, but when you can fully comprehend God's deeply personal care for you, his love breaks through your feelings of loneliness and tends to your deepest needs and worries.

DIVINE PROMISE

THE LORD IS CLOSE TO ALL WHO CALL ON HIM, YES, TO ALL WHO CALL ON HIM IN TRUTH. HE GRANTS THE DESIRES OF THOSE WHO FEAR HIM; HE HEARS THEIR CRIES FOR HELP AND RESCUES THEM. THE LORD PROTECTS ALL THOSE WHO LOVE HIM, BUT HE DESTROYS THE WICKED.   *Psalm 145:18-20*

Challenges

MY QUESTION *for* GOD

How can challenges shape my life?

A MOMENT *with* GOD

Dear brothers and sisters, when troubles come your way, consider it an opportunity for great joy. For you know that when your faith is tested, your endurance has a chance to grow. So let it grow, for when your endurance is fully developed, you will be perfect and complete, needing nothing.   JAMES 1:2-4

I have traveled on many long journeys. I have faced danger from rivers and from robbers. I have faced danger from my own people, the Jews, as well as from the Gentiles. I have faced danger in the cities, in the deserts, and on the seas. And I have faced danger from men who claim to be believers but are not.

2 CORINTHIANS 11:26

Paul's vision to preach the gospel in new places continually drove him to new challenges and therefore to greater growth in his relationship with God. God has called you, too, to do something for him. Just as it takes the rough surface of a file to sharpen and smooth the blade of a knife, so it takes rough times to sharpen you into the kind of person that God can use effectively. Any challenge is a tool God can use to hone you, bringing you greater wisdom, more maturity to withstand the knocks and hits that come your way, and the ability to cut through life's obstacles. As you endure these challenges, you gain more and more courage to face whatever comes your way. Accepting life's challenges will force you to follow God's leading into uncharted waters so that you can accomplish something unique and purposeful for him.

DIVINE PROMISE

BE STRONG AND COURAGEOUS, AND DO THE WORK. DON'T BE AFRAID OR DISCOURAGED, FOR THE LORD GOD, MY GOD, IS WITH YOU. HE WILL NOT FAIL YOU OR FORSAKE YOU. HE WILL SEE TO IT THAT ALL THE WORK RELATED TO THE TEMPLE OF THE LORD IS FINISHED CORRECTLY.   *1 Chronicles 28:20*

Change

MY QUESTION *for* GOD

How can I find security and peace in the midst of change?

A MOMENT *with* GOD

LORD, you remain the same forever! Your throne continues from generation to generation.

LAMENTATIONS 5:19

I am the LORD, and I do not change.   MALACHI 3:6

Jesus Christ is the same yesterday, today, and forever. So do not be attracted by strange, new ideas. Your strength comes from God's grace.   HEBREWS 13:8-9

If there's one thing you can count on, it's change! Sometimes change is expected, even anticipated. Sometimes it is the result of tragedy or unexpected circumstances. It doesn't matter whether the change is something we welcome or dread, change always rocks the boat of life for a while. During any time of change, it's important to have an anchor and a plan. Anchoring yourself to others, your job, or your accomplishments only makes you less secure. When the waves come, your life will fall apart and wash away. But if your life is anchored to God and your plan is to obey him, true peace is possible no matter what the change. Since God is unchanging and eternal, obedience to him is the best way to find rock-solid security when you are in troubled waters. Even when circumstances change your neatly laid plans, you will still find peace in obeying God.

DIVINE PROMISE

HEAVEN AND EARTH WILL DISAPPEAR, BUT MY WORDS WILL NEVER DISAPPEAR. *Mark 13:31*

Children

MY QUESTION for GOD

What lessons can we learn from children?

A MOMENT *with* GOD

Jesus called a little child to him. . . . Then he said, "I tell you the truth, unless you turn from your sins and become like little children, you will never get into the Kingdom of Heaven."

MATTHEW 18:2-3

When Jesus saw what was happening . . . he said to them, "Let the children come to me. Don't stop them! For the Kingdom of God belongs to those who are like these children. I tell you the truth, anyone who doesn't receive the Kingdom of God like a child will never enter it." Then he took the children in his arms and placed his hands on their heads and blessed them.

MARK 10:14-16

Children have a way of approaching life with delight. They have not yet been weighed down with the burdens and problems of living or jaded by hurt and rejection. Children simply see the world as fresh, carefree, and full of adventure. Jesus loved this quality in children, and he urged adults to follow their example. When you approach God, do you come with an agenda of business to take care of, or do you simply take delight in his love? Do you fight obedience to God in your spirit, or are you ready for the adventure of following God? When you can simply enjoy God and all he created, you will find joy in living. God planned childhood not just for the child, but also for the parents.

DIVINE PROMISE

YOU WILL TAKE DELIGHT IN THE ALMIGHTY AND LOOK UP TO GOD. *Job 22:26*

Choices

MY QUESTION *for* GOD

How can I know I'm making the right choices in life?

A MOMENT *with* GOD

Fools think their own way is right, but the wise listen to others. PROVERBS 12:15

Fear of the LORD is the foundation of true knowledge, but fools despise wisdom and discipline. PROVERBS 1:7

He guides me along right paths, bringing honor to his name. PSALM 23:3

Why do the right choices often seem the hardest to make? Right choices are always consistent with God's Word. He will never lead you to a sinful choice. When you know the right thing to do, God will confirm it deep in your heart, and other trustworthy people around you will agree. It may not make it any easier, but knowing what is right can help give you the courage to do it. The Bible calls this wisdom, and true wisdom comes from the Word of God.

DIVINE PROMISE

IF YOU NEED WISDOM, ASK OUR GENEROUS
GOD, AND HE WILL GIVE IT TO YOU. HE WILL
NOT REBUKE YOU FOR ASKING. BUT WHEN YOU
ASK HIM, BE SURE THAT YOUR FAITH IS IN GOD
ALONE. DO NOT WAVER, FOR A PERSON WITH
DIVIDED LOYALTY IS AS UNSETTLED AS A WAVE
OF THE SEA THAT IS BLOWN AND TOSSED BY
THE WIND.   *James 1:5-6*

Church

MY QUESTION *for* GOD

How can I experience God by going to church?

A MOMENT *with* GOD

The one thing I ask of the LORD—the thing I seek
most—is to live in the house of the LORD all the days
of my life, delighting in the LORD's perfections and
meditating in his Temple.   PSALM 27:4

What joy for those who can live in your house, always
singing your praises.   PSALM 84:4

Even though God lives in the heart of every believer,
he also lives in the community of the church. When
the church gathers together, it meets God in a special
way. In the same way that actually being at a concert or
sports event is much more exciting than just watching
it on television, participating with other believers in

worship is much more meaningful than trying to worship on your own.

Just as our bodies have many parts and each part has a special function, so it is with Christ's body. We are many parts of one body, and we all belong to each other.   ROMANS 12:4-5

*G*od has given every believer special gifts—some are great organizers and administrators, while others are gifted musicians, teachers, and dishwashers! When everyone in the congregation uses their gifts to serve, the church becomes a powerful force for good, a strong witness for Jesus, and a mighty army to combat Satan's attacks against God's people. The church needs you, for the body of Christ is not complete unless you are there!

Let us not neglect our meeting together, as some people do, but encourage one another, especially now that the day of his return is drawing near.

HEBREWS 10:25

*G*ood friends are a wonderful gift, but fellowship at church among other believers is unique because almighty God is in your midst. The church brings people together who have a common perspective on life. Christian fellowship provides a place of honest sharing about the things that really matter, encouragement to stay strong in the face of temptation and persecution, and godly wisdom to help you deal with problems you may be facing.

DIVINE PROMISE

WHERE TWO OR THREE GATHER TOGETHER AS MY FOLLOWERS, I AM THERE AMONG THEM.

Matthew 18:20

Comfort

MY QUESTION *for* GOD

In my times of distress, how does God comfort me?

A MOMENT *with* GOD

I meditate on your age-old regulations; O LORD, they comfort me.   PSALM 119:52

Whenever they were in trouble and turned to the LORD, the God of Israel, and sought him out, they found him.   2 CHRONICLES 15:4

The LORD is good, a strong refuge when trouble comes. He is close to those who trust in him.   NAHUM 1:7

God doesn't always act in the way you might expect. You might expect God to comfort you by providing you with the things that you think you want or need, but the Bible says that God often comforts you with his presence, not with provisions. Things are temporary; your needs and wants are constantly changing, but God is permanent and eternal. While material provisions can provide comfort for a time, God is the only source who can shower you with his comfort at all times. God shows up every time you need comfort—not with presents but with his *presence*. It is God's presence, and knowing he is beside you, that settles your soul in the moments of your very worst distress.

DIVINE PROMISE

DON'T BE AFRAID, FOR I AM WITH YOU. DON'T BE DISCOURAGED, FOR I AM YOUR GOD. I WILL STRENGTHEN YOU AND HELP YOU. I WILL HOLD YOU UP WITH MY VICTORIOUS RIGHT HAND. *Isaiah 41:10*

Communication

MY QUESTIONS *for* GOD

I've heard people say that God spoke to them. Does God really talk to people? How can I know if he's speaking to me?

A MOMENT *with* GOD

Devote yourselves to prayer with an alert mind and a thankful heart. COLOSSIANS 4:2

Elijah replied, "I have zealously served the LORD God Almighty. But the people of Israel have broken their covenant with you, torn down your altars, and killed every one of your prophets. I am the only one left, and now they are trying to kill me, too." "Go out and stand before me on the mountain," the LORD told him. And as Elijah stood there, the LORD passed by, and a mighty windstorm hit the mountain. It was such a terrible blast that the rocks were torn loose, but the LORD was not in the wind. After the wind there was an earthquake, but the LORD was not in the earthquake. And after the earthquake there was a fire, but the LORD was not in the fire. And after the fire there was the sound of a gentle whisper. When Elijah heard it, he wrapped his face in his cloak and went out and stood at the entrance of the cave. And a voice said, "What are you doing here, Elijah?"

1 KINGS 19:10-13

God does communicate with his people—just not always in an audible voice. While you might prefer to hear a voice booming from heaven, God more often communicates with you in less obvious ways. If God only talked to you and told you everything you needed to know up front, the relationship with him would be one-sided, with God always initiating communication with you. God doesn't always communicate in obvious ways because he wants you to come to him as a demonstration that your faith in him is genuine. The key is being prepared to hear God speak, and most often he speaks to you in the quietness of your own heart. If you are too busy rushing through life at a frantic pace, you will miss hearing God. If you really want God to speak to you, set aside some quiet time in your day to focus on hearing what he is saying to you.

DIVINE PROMISE

COME CLOSE TO GOD, AND GOD WILL COME
CLOSE TO YOU.   *James 4:8*

Compassion

MY QUESTION *for* GOD

How is my compassion for others related to my faith?

A MOMENT *with* GOD

The LORD is like a father to his children, tender and
compassionate to those who fear him.   PSALM 103:13

He will rescue the poor when they cry to him; he
will help the oppressed, who have no one to defend
them. He feels pity for the weak and the needy, and
he will rescue them. He will redeem them from
oppression and violence, for their lives are precious
to him.   PSALM 72:12-14

Moved with compassion, Jesus reached out and
touched him.   MARK 1:41

You must be compassionate, just as your Father is
compassionate.   LUKE 6:36

Your level of compassion is a litmus test of your commitment and desire to love others as Christ loves you.
To be Christlike is to share in his compassionate feelings toward the needy, particularly those who cannot

help themselves. Often the best way to experience Christ's compassion for you is to show compassion for others. When your heart truly aches for another, you get an idea of how the needs of all humanity moved Jesus to die on the cross. If you're not moved by the incredible needs and hurts around you, you are either too self-focused or are in danger of developing a heart of stone, which will soon become unresponsive to God or others.

DIVINE PROMISE

THE LORD IS MERCIFUL AND COMPASSIONATE, SLOW TO GET ANGRY AND FILLED WITH UNFAILING LOVE. THE LORD IS GOOD TO EVERYONE. HE SHOWERS COMPASSION ON ALL HIS CREATION.   *Psalm 145:8-9*

Compromise

MY QUESTION *for* GOD

How do I live in today's culture without compromising my convictions?

A MOMENT *with* GOD

Daniel was determined not to defile himself by eating the food. . . . He asked . . . permission not to eat these unacceptable foods. . . . "Please test us for ten days on a diet of vegetables and water," Daniel said. . . . The attendant agreed to Daniel's suggestion and tested them for ten days. At the end of the ten days, Daniel . . . looked healthier and better nourished than the young men who had been eating the food assigned by the king. DANIEL 1:8, 12-15

Be very careful never to make a treaty with the people who live in the land where you are going. If you do, you will follow their evil ways and be trapped. EXODUS 34:12

There is a time to compromise and a time to stand firm. When the forces of evil want their way, you cannot budge. To compromise God's truth, God's ways, or God's Word is to negotiate with that which is unholy. The test of acceptable compromise is simple: Can two parties reach a mutually satisfactory agreement without either party having to sacrifice his or her beliefs about what is right? To give up godliness for anything is a bad bargain. You lose, and Satan wins. When you refuse to compromise your convictions, you will experience a divine moment, and you will sense God's peace, knowing that you have done the right thing.

DIVINE PROMISE

PUT ON ALL OF GOD'S ARMOR SO THAT YOU WILL BE ABLE TO STAND FIRM AGAINST ALL STRATEGIES OF THE DEVIL. *Ephesians 6:11*

Confession

MY QUESTION *for* GOD

Why do I ever need to confess anything to anyone?

A MOMENT *with* GOD

If my people who are called by my name will humble themselves and pray and seek my face and turn from their wicked ways, I will hear from heaven and will forgive their sins and restore their land. 2 CHRONICLES 7:14

I confessed all my sins to you and stopped trying to hide my guilt. I said to myself, "I will confess my rebellion to the LORD." And you forgave me! All my guilt is gone. PSALM 32:5

Confess your sins to each other and pray for each other so that you may be healed. JAMES 5:16

Confession is the acknowledgment of guilt to other people or to God. It is embarrassing and sometimes painful to acknowledge the ugliness of a sin you've committed. Perhaps the embarrassment is in letting others see deeply into your life, of being vulnerable to the possibility of being ridiculed. But confession is a necessary part of knowing God, of being released from guilt through his forgiveness, and of finding new beginnings.

DIVINE PROMISE

PEOPLE WHO CONCEAL THEIR SINS WILL NOT PROSPER, BUT IF THEY CONFESS AND TURN FROM THEM, THEY WILL RECEIVE MERCY.

Proverbs 28:13

Confidence

MY QUESTIONS *for* GOD

How can I develop confidence in God? What happens if I lose it?

A MOMENT *with* GOD

The LORD is my light and my salvation—so why should I be afraid? The LORD is my fortress, protecting me from danger, so why should I tremble?   PSALM 27:1

The LORD keeps watch over you as you come and go, both now and forever.   PSALM 121:8

Many great athletes say that their real contest is more mental than physical. The same can be said of your spiritual life. Your confidence comes not from your physical circumstances (how you look or what you achieve), but from the inner assurance that God is by your side, making his wisdom and power available to you and working out his purpose for your life. When you begin to lose confidence in God, go to his promises in the Bible. As you remember the ones he has already fulfilled and take comfort from those, your confidence in him will grow.

DIVINE PROMISE

I CAN DO EVERYTHING THROUGH CHRIST, WHO GIVES ME STRENGTH. *Philippians 4:13*

Conflict

MY QUESTION *for* GOD

What is the best way to respond to conflict?

A MOMENT *with* GOD

Dear friends, never take revenge. Leave that to the righteous anger of God. For the Scriptures say, "I will take revenge; I will pay them back," says the LORD. Instead, "If your enemies are hungry, feed them. If they are thirsty, give them something to drink. In doing this, you will heap burning coals of shame on their heads." Don't let evil conquer you, but conquer evil by doing good. ROMANS 12:19-21

Don't repay evil for evil. Don't retaliate with insults when people insult you. Instead, pay them back with a blessing. That is what God has called you to do, and he will bless you for it. . . . Search for peace, and work to maintain it. 1 PETER 3:9-11

You have heard the law that says, "Love your neighbor" and hate your enemy. But I say, love your enemies! Pray for those who persecute you! In that way, you will be acting as true children of your Father in heaven.

MATTHEW 5:43-45

*T*he path to peace lies in the power of love, not in the love of power. Followers of God know better than to take revenge into their own hands. They know that fighting according to the world's ways continues the cycle of conflict. Instead, practice the "principle of paradox": Bless your enemy, give when you feel threatened, and feed those who would take your food. Following this principle in a situation of conflict unleashes God's power, which can resolve conflict that from a human standpoint could not be solved.

DIVINE PROMISE

GOD BLESSES THOSE WHO WORK FOR PEACE, FOR THEY WILL BE CALLED THE CHILDREN OF GOD. *Matthew 5:9*

Confusion

MY QUESTION *for* GOD

How should I respond when I'm confused about what God wants me to do?

A MOMENT *with* GOD

Let us hold tightly without wavering to the hope we affirm, for God can be trusted to keep his promise.

HEBREWS 10:23

This is what the LORD says—the Holy One of Israel and your Creator: "Do you question what I do for my children? Do you give me orders about the work of my hands?"

ISAIAH 45:11

Fix your thoughts on what is true, and honorable, and right, and pure, and lovely, and admirable. Think about things that are excellent and worthy of praise. Keep putting into practice all you learned and received from me—everything you heard from me and saw me doing. Then the God of peace will be with you.

PHILIPPIANS 4:8-9

Confusion comes when you waver, or it can cause you to waver when you are uncertain about which road to take. But you will be hopelessly confused if you don't even know what you are looking for at the end of the road. If you take God's Word as your compass for life, you will at least be certain about what roads not to take. That's a great place to begin reducing the confusion in your life. When you begin to doubt that you want what God wants, read his Word, focus your thoughts on him, and pray for his wisdom. It will become clear what he wants you to do and what he wants you to avoid. Much of your confusion will clear up when you view the world from God's perspective.

DIVINE PROMISE

THE LORD IS GOD, AND HE CREATED THE
HEAVENS AND EARTH AND PUT EVERYTHING
IN PLACE. HE MADE THE WORLD TO BE LIVED
IN, NOT TO BE A PLACE OF EMPTY CHAOS. "I AM
THE LORD," HE SAYS, "AND THERE IS NO OTHER."

Isaiah 45:18

Conscience

MY QUESTION *for* GOD

How does my conscience work?

A MOMENT *with* GOD

They know the truth about God because he has
made it obvious to them. For ever since the world
was created, people have seen the earth and sky.
Through everything God made, they can clearly see
his invisible qualities—his eternal power and divine
nature. So they have no excuse for not knowing God.

ROMANS 1:19-20

Cling to your faith in Christ, and keep your
conscience clear. For some people have deliberately
violated their consciences; as a result, their faith has
been shipwrecked.   1 TIMOTHY 1:19

They knew God, but they wouldn't worship him
as God or even give him thanks. And they began to

think up foolish ideas of what God was like. As a result, their minds became dark and confused.

ROMANS 1:21

Conscience is the innate part of you that helps you understand whether or not you are in line with God's will. It is God's gift to keep each person sensitive to his moral code. But you must use the gift. If you don't listen to and obey your conscience, it will become less sensitive and harder to hear. In addition, it will malfunction if you don't care for it properly. It can become a flawed witness that may either condemn you too harshly or let you off too easily. Your conscience will function effectively only when you stay close to God, spend time in his Word, and make an effort to understand yourself and your own tendencies toward sin. If your conscience is working faithfully, it will activate your heart and mind to distinguish right from wrong. You will have a strong inner sense, a voice of accountability, about doing what is right. If you have a reputation for not always doing the right thing or if you find yourself unmoved by evil, it may be an indication that your conscience has become dull or inactive. If so, ask God, through his holy Word to sharpen and resensitize your conscience. Then it will speak to you in concert with God himself.

DIVINE PROMISE

MY CHILD, LISTEN TO WHAT I SAY. . . . THEN
YOU WILL UNDERSTAND WHAT IS RIGHT, JUST,
AND FAIR, AND YOU WILL FIND THE RIGHT
WAY TO GO.   *Proverbs 2:1, 9*

Consequences

MY QUESTION *for* GOD

What is the value of thinking through an issue before acting?

A MOMENT *with* GOD

To [Adam, God] said, "Since you . . . ate from the
tree whose fruit I commanded you not to eat, the
ground is cursed because of you. All your life you
will struggle to scratch a living from it."   GENESIS 3:17

The tongue can bring death or life; those who love to
talk will reap the consequences.   PROVERBS 18:21

Those who live only to satisfy their own sinful nature
will harvest decay and death from that sinful nature.
But those who live to please the Spirit will harvest
everlasting life from the Spirit.   GALATIANS 6:8

You will always harvest what you plant.   GALATIANS 6:7

A gun fires, a bullet is released, and a person in its
path dies. That death is the consequence of someone's
pulling the trigger of a loaded weapon. Similarly,

someone speaks words that wound another person. Those wounds are the consequence of the speaker's harsh or damaging words. Someone else speaks loving and gracious words, and the hearer is drawn to Christ. That, too, is a consequence of words, but those are words that serve God. The word *consequence* means an outcome, aftermath, or result. With some actions the consequences are neither morally good nor bad (for example, if you take a shower you will get clean). But many thoughts and actions have definite good or bad consequences. Sin causes bad consequences—always. Faithfulness to God results in good consequences—always. Before you act, think—what will the consequences of my actions be?

DIVINE PROMISE

PLANT THE GOOD SEEDS OF RIGHTEOUSNESS, AND YOU WILL HARVEST A CROP OF LOVE. PLOW UP THE HARD GROUND OF YOUR HEARTS, FOR NOW IS THE TIME TO SEEK THE LORD, THAT HE MAY COME AND SHOWER RIGHTEOUSNESS UPON YOU.   *Hosea 10:12*

Contentment

MY QUESTION *for* GOD

How can I find contentment regardless of life's circumstances?

A Moment *with* God

Don't love money; be satisfied with what you have.
For God has said, "I will never fail you. I will never
abandon you."   HEBREWS 13:5

I have learned how to be content with whatever I
have. I know how to live on almost nothing or with
everything. I have learned the secret of living in every
situation, whether it is with a full stomach or empty,
with plenty or little. For I can do everything through
Christ, who gives me strength.   PHILIPPIANS 4:11-13

*M*ost of us tend to equate contentment with having
all we need and want to be happy. No wonder we get
rattled when life goes sour and material wealth doesn't
satisfy. True contentment has nothing to do with having material goods and enjoying perfect circumstances.
True contentment happens only through the peace and
love God offers, and it stays secure despite life's circumstances. Contentment settles in your heart when
you meditate on God's Word, and give him control of
your life.

DIVINE PROMISE

YOU WILL KEEP IN PERFECT PEACE ALL WHO
TRUST IN YOU, ALL WHOSE THOUGHTS ARE
FIXED ON YOU!   *Isaiah 26:3*

Conviction

MY QUESTIONS *for* GOD

What is conviction? Why is it important?

A MOMENT *with* GOD

You must continue to believe this truth and stand
firmly in it. Don't drift away from the assurance you
received when you heard the Good News.

COLOSSIANS 1:23

You may believe there's nothing wrong with what
you are doing, but keep it between yourself and
God. Blessed are those who don't feel guilty for
doing something they have decided is right. But if
you have doubts about whether or not you should eat
something, you are sinning if you go ahead and do it.
For you are not following your convictions. If you do
anything you believe is not right, you are sinning.

ROMANS 14:22-23

Daniel was determined not to defile himself by eating
the food and wine given to them by the king. He
asked the chief of staff for permission not to eat these
unacceptable foods.   DANIEL 1:8

Conviction is more than just a belief; it is a commitment to a belief. What you think, say, and do shows
the level of your conviction. For example, if you believe God exists and created you, then out of this belief
should come the commitment to live by his Word, to

serve others, and to fulfill his purpose for your life. Convictions prepare you to effectively live a life of faith and to defend your faith when necessary. Keep your convictions sharp, and your life will be a great story of faith in God.

DIVINE PROMISE

BECAUSE THE SOVEREIGN LORD HELPS ME, I WILL NOT BE DISGRACED. THEREFORE, I HAVE SET MY FACE LIKE A STONE, DETERMINED TO DO HIS WILL. AND I KNOW THAT I WILL NOT BE PUT TO SHAME. *Isaiah 50:7*

Courage

MY QUESTIONS *for* GOD

Where can I find the courage to do the right thing? Where can I find the courage to go on when life seems too hard?

A MOMENT *with* GOD

The LORD your God . . . is with you!

DEUTERONOMY 20:1

The LORD is my light and my salvation—so why should I be afraid?   PSALM 27:1

Don't be afraid, for I am with you. Don't be discouraged, for I am your God. I will strengthen you and help you. I will hold you up with my victorious right hand.

ISAIAH 41:10

Throughout your life you will find yourself in scary situations—mortal danger, extreme stress, major illness, financial hardship, or any number of other problems. True courage comes from understanding that God is stronger than your biggest problem or your worst enemy and that he wants you to use his power to help you. Courage is not misplaced confidence in your own strength; it is well-placed confidence in God's strength. Fear comes from feeling alone against a great threat. Courage comes from knowing that God is beside you, helping you fight the threat. To stay courageous, focus more on God's power and less on your problem.

DIVINE PROMISE

THIS IS MY COMMAND—BE STRONG AND COURAGEOUS! DO NOT BE AFRAID OR DISCOURAGED. FOR THE LORD YOUR GOD IS WITH YOU WHEREVER YOU GO. *Joshua 1:9*

Crisis

MY QUESTION *for* GOD

Where is God in my time of crisis?

A MOMENT *with* GOD

By means of their suffering, he rescues those who suffer. For he gets their attention through adversity.

JOB 36:15

The LORD hears the cries of the needy; he does not despise his imprisoned people.   PSALM 69:33

Can anything ever separate us from Christ's love? Does it mean he no longer loves us if we have trouble or calamity, or are persecuted, or hungry, or destitute, or in danger, or threatened with death?

ROMANS 8:35

I have told you all this so that you may have peace in me. Here on earth you will have many trials and sorrows. But take heart, because I have overcome the world.   JOHN 16:33

*Y*ou need not pray for God to be with you in times of crisis—he already is. Instead, pray that you will recognize his presence and have the humility and discernment to accept his help. God does not say he will always prevent crises in your life—this is a world where terrible things happen. But God does promise to be there with you and for you—always—helping you through any crisis. He promises to guide you toward peace and hope in the midst of crisis. And he also promises to bring you to a place—heaven—where all trouble will end forever. Too often we become so focused on the present that we forget it is such a tiny part of our eternity. When a crisis arises and you feel yourself beginning to panic, pray not that God will be with you but that you will recognize his presence and can experience peace of mind and heart.

DIVINE PROMISE

GOD IS OUR REFUGE AND STRENGTH, ALWAYS
READY TO HELP IN TIMES OF TROUBLE. SO WE
WILL NOT FEAR WHEN EARTHQUAKES COME
AND THE MOUNTAINS CRUMBLE INTO THE SEA.
LET THE OCEANS ROAR AND FOAM. LET THE
MOUNTAINS TREMBLE AS THE WATERS SURGE!

Psalm 46:1-3

Culture

MY QUESTION *for* GOD

How does culture affect me?

A MOMENT *with* GOD

Don't copy the behavior and customs of this world,
but let God transform you into a new person by
changing the way you think. Then you will learn to
know God's will for you, which is good and pleasing
and perfect.   ROMANS 12:2

Every day the weather affects your life. The tempera-
ture, precipitation, wind and other factors all affect
what you choose to do and even what you wear. The
weather can even affect your attitude. If it is dark and
gloomy, you may feel depressed or weary. If it is a bril-
liant, sunny day, you might feel energetic and joyful.
Adjusting to the weather is something you hardly notice
unless you stop to think about it. Similarly, culture also
affects you far more than you realize. It has an impact

on almost everything you do. Culture plays a subtle but important role in influencing your values, beliefs, and actions. The culture in which you live takes on a personality of its own, pressuring you to conform and fit in, challenging what you believe, and even shaming you into compliance. As a result, without even realizing it, you may be copying lifestyle choices that are disappointing to God. To follow God's will, you have to know it by becoming familiar with his Word. Your life can be transformed when God helps you to challenge your worldview and change the way you think about your culture and respond to it.

DIVINE CHALLENGE

YOU ARE THE LIGHT OF THE WORLD—LIKE A CITY ON A HILLTOP THAT CANNOT BE HIDDEN. NO ONE LIGHTS A LAMP AND THEN PUTS IT UNDER A BASKET. INSTEAD, A LAMP IS PLACED ON A STAND, WHERE IT GIVES LIGHT TO EVERYONE IN THE HOUSE. IN THE SAME WAY, LET YOUR GOOD DEEDS SHINE OUT FOR ALL TO SEE, SO THAT EVERYONE WILL PRAISE YOUR HEAVENLY FATHER. *Matthew 5:14-16*

Danger

MY QUESTION *for* GOD

What is one danger I must constantly be aware of?

A Moment *with* God

Dear children, keep away from anything that might
take God's place in your hearts.   1 JOHN 5:21

Stay alert! Watch out for your great enemy, the devil.
He prowls around like a roaring lion, looking for
someone to devour.   1 PETER 5:8

Temptation to do wrong is one of the greatest dangers
you will face. The purpose of a guardrail on a dangerous curve is not to inhibit your freedom to drive but
to save your life! That guardrail is a sign of security
and safety, not an obstacle to flying. In the same way,
you need a guardrail as you travel through life—not to
inhibit your freedom but to help you avoid danger and
keep your life from going out of control. Your heart
determines where you go because it most affects your
passions. If you don't guard your heart with God's
Word and stay focused on the road God has put you
on, you may have a terrible accident when temptation
distracts you. Satan is constantly on the attack, trying
to tempt you to sin against God. You will give in from
time to time—every human does—but caution will
help you be aware of temptation so that you can recognize it, admit it, and avoid it. When you throw caution
to the wind, you will likely give in to temptation at
every whim, and then you will be in danger of being
completely ineffective for God.

THE WISE ARE CAUTIOUS AND AVOID DANGER;
FOOLS PLUNGE AHEAD WITH RECKLESS
CONFIDENCE.   *Proverbs 14:16*

Death

MY QUESTION *for* GOD

Is fear of death or thinking about death a bad thing?

A MOMENT *with* GOD

Teach us to realize the brevity of life, so that we may
grow in wisdom.   PSALM 90:12

Since you have been raised to new life with Christ,
set your sights on the realities of heaven. . . . Think
about the things of heaven, not the things of earth.

COLOSSIANS 3:1-2

Don't be afraid of those who want to kill your body;
they cannot touch your soul.   MATTHEW 10:28

Jesus told her, "I am the resurrection and the life.
Anyone who believes in me will live, even after
dying."   JOHN 11:25

*I*t's not unusual to be afraid of something you have
never experienced before, but an inordinate fear of death
or spending an unreasonable amount of time thinking
about it may be an indication of a weak relationship

with God, a misunderstanding about heaven, a lack of
perspective that what you do here affects how you live
there, or a lack of trust in God's promises. Take time
to learn what the Bible says about heaven. Trust God's
assurances about what eternity is like for those who
love Jesus, and apply yourself to knowing and serving
God more and more. The more real God is to you, the
less fearsome death will be.

DIVINE PROMISE

IT IS THE SAME WAY WITH THE RESURRECTION
OF THE DEAD. OUR EARTHLY BODIES ARE
PLANTED IN THE GROUND WHEN WE DIE, BUT
THEY WILL BE RAISED TO LIVE FOREVER.
1 Corinthians 15:42

Deception

MY QUESTION for GOD

In what ways do I deceive myself?

A MOMENT with GOD

The human heart is the most deceitful of all things.

JEREMIAH 17:9

Don't be misled—you cannot mock the justice of
God. You will always harvest what you plant. Those
who live only to satisfy their own sinful nature will
harvest decay and death from that sinful nature.

But those who live to please the Spirit will harvest
everlasting life from the Spirit.   GALATIANS 6:7-8

Stop deceiving yourselves. If you think you are wise
by this world's standards, you need to become a fool
to be truly wise. For the wisdom of this world is
foolishness to God.   1 CORINTHIANS 3:18-19

*Y*ou deceive yourself if you think you can disobey
God and not suffer the consequences or that you can
ignore him and still receive his blessings. When you
live as if this world is all there is, you deceive yourself.
Sooner or later, these deceptions will catch up with
you. Don't let materialism and the pursuit of pleasure
blind you to the realities of God's wisdom, guidance,
holiness, and justice. When your heart is open to God's
Word, his truth breaks through to help you see your
life from his perspective.

DIVINE PROMISE

WHAT JOY FOR THOSE WHOSE RECORD THE
LORD HAS CLEARED OF GUILT, WHOSE LIVES
ARE LIVED IN COMPLETE HONESTY! *Psalm 32:2*

Defeat

MY QUESTION *for* GOD

What can I learn from defeat?

A Moment *with* God

If your people Israel are defeated by their enemies because they have sinned against you, and if they turn to you and acknowledge your name and pray to you here in this Temple, then hear from heaven and forgive the sin of your people Israel and return them to this land you gave their ancestors.   1 KINGS 8:33-34

I used to wander off until you disciplined me; but now I closely follow your word. . . . My suffering was good for me, for it taught me to pay attention to your decrees.   PSALM 119:67, 71

We think you ought to know, dear brothers and sisters, about the trouble we went through in the province of Asia. We were crushed and overwhelmed beyond our ability to endure, and we thought we would never live through it. In fact, we expected to die. But as a result, we stopped relying on ourselves and learned to rely only on God, who raises the dead. And he did rescue us from mortal danger, and he will rescue us again. We have placed our confidence in him, and he will continue to rescue us.   2 CORINTHIANS 1:8-10

Humble yourselves under the mighty power of God, and at the right time he will lift you up in honor.

1 PETER 5:6

Expecting to win all the time is not realistic or even healthy for you. It will not train you to overcome adversity or to persevere through trouble. If you win all the time, your character has no chance to grow, and you may become proud and arrogant and rely only on yourself with no regard for others' opinions or help. Failing from time to time keeps you humble and dependent on God. Defeat is a common denominator of all people and will keep you connected with the realities all of us face. Allow God to use times of defeat to grow your character and keep you humbly reliant on him.

DIVINE PROMISE

THE LORD IS MY STRENGTH AND MY SONG; HE HAS GIVEN ME VICTORY.   *Exodus 15:2*

Demons

MY QUESTIONS *for* GOD

Are demons real? Are they powerful? Is there help for us against them?

A MOMENT *with* GOD

We are not fighting against flesh-and-blood enemies, but against evil rulers and authorities of the unseen world, against mighty powers in this dark world, and against evil spirits in the heavenly places.   EPHESIANS 6:12

These people are false apostles. They are deceitful workers who disguise themselves as apostles of Christ. But I am not surprised! Even Satan disguises himself as an angel of light. So it is no wonder that his servants also disguise themselves as servants

of righteousness. In the end they will get the
punishment their wicked deeds deserve.

2 CORINTHIANS 11:13-15

Stay alert! Watch out for your great enemy, the devil.
He prowls around like a roaring lion, looking for
someone to devour. Stand firm against him, and be
strong in your faith.   1 PETER 5:8-9

Demons are real. Although you cannot see them,
you can see the ways in which their evil is manifested.
These demons, motivated by Satan, are always on the
attack. Their intentions are to harm, to destroy, and
to turn people away from God. They are powerful,
they don't play fair, and they are not above attacking
you in your weakest moments. But there is a greater
reality: God has already defeated them, and they are
subject to his authority. Demons have limited power,
and the Bible describes them as cowering before God in
fear. Therefore, if you believe in God, you have God's
power, strength, and authority over demons.

DIVINE PROMISE

I AM CONVINCED THAT NOTHING CAN EVER
SEPARATE US FROM GOD'S LOVE. NEITHER
DEATH NOR LIFE, NEITHER ANGELS NOR
DEMONS . . . NOT EVEN THE POWERS OF HELL
CAN SEPARATE US FROM GOD'S LOVE.   *Romans 8:38*

Denial

MY QUESTIONS *for* GOD

Is denial ever a good thing? What kind of denial does God want from me?

A MOMENT *with* GOD

Those who belong to Christ Jesus have nailed the passions and desires of their sinful nature to his cross and crucified them there. Since we are living by the Spirit, let us follow the Spirit's leading in every part of our lives. Let us not become conceited. GALATIANS 5:24-26

You cannot become my disciple without giving up everything you own. LUKE 14:33

Everything else is worthless when compared with the infinite value of knowing Christ Jesus my Lord. For his sake I have discarded everything else, counting it all as garbage, so that I could gain Christ and become one with him. PHILIPPIANS 3:8-9

God calls you to exercise restraint and self-discipline in the way you live. This means you must deny any self-centered attitudes for the sake of obeying him. You will need to give up some things in order to prevent you from giving up on God. If asked, would you be willing to give up everything for God? He may not ask you to do something that dramatic, but he loves that kind of attitude in his followers.

DIVINE PROMISE

IF YOU TRY TO HANG ON TO YOUR LIFE, YOU
WILL LOSE IT. BUT IF YOU GIVE UP YOUR LIFE
FOR MY SAKE, YOU WILL SAVE IT.   *Matthew 16:25*

Dependence

MY QUESTION *for* GOD

What does it mean to depend on God?

A MOMENT *with* GOD

I said to the LORD, "You are my Master! Every good
thing I have comes from you."   PSALM 16:2

O our God, we thank you and praise your glorious
name! But who am I, and who are my people, that we
could give anything to you? Everything we have has
come from you, and we give you only what you first
gave us!   1 CHRONICLES 29:13-14

Depending on God is recognizing him as the source
of your strength, of your successes, and of all good
things in your life. Everything you have ultimately
comes from his hand of mercy. Since he created you,
he knows you inside and out, so you can depend on him
to guide you into what is best for you. Dependence on
God, who knows you and cares about you, is the secret
to living the most fulfilling life possible.

DIVINE PROMISE

DEEP IN YOUR HEARTS YOU KNOW THAT
EVERY PROMISE OF THE LORD YOUR GOD
HAS COME TRUE. NOT A SINGLE ONE
HAS FAILED!   *Joshua 23:14*

Depression

MY QUESTION *for* GOD

Does feeling depressed mean something is wrong with my faith?

A MOMENT *with* GOD

I have told you these things so that you will be filled
with my joy. Yes, your joy will overflow!   JOHN 15:11

Those who listen to instruction will prosper; those
who trust the LORD will be joyful.   PROVERBS 16:20

God does not regard depression as sin, nor does he
take it lightly. Rather, he responds to those who suffer
its darkness with great tenderness, understanding, and
compassion.

When you are depressed, the Bible helps you recognize the lies of Satan, the temptations that will come
your way, and how the devil fuels your depression by
distracting you from God's promises and power. As
these things become clear, your perspective may begin
to change. Develop the regular habit of seeking God

and counting on his Word to be true, and you will find
encouragement to help you as you battle depression.

Samson was now very thirsty, and he cried out to the
LORD, "You have accomplished this great victory.
. . . Must I now die of thirst?"   JUDGES 15:18

Elijah was afraid and fled for his life. . . . . He sat
down under a solitary broom tree and prayed that he
might die.   1 KINGS 19:3-4

*E*ven for the people of God, depression can follow
great achievement or spiritual victory. You are on such
a high that the only place to go is down. If you recognize this, you will not be surprised when you feel down
soon after feeling on top of the world. This is normal.
But beware of the common tendency to neglect God
after a spiritual victory. Instead, fill your heart and
mind with God's Word, which will encourage you
with God's love and care while you battle feelings of
depression.

DIVINE PROMISE

EVEN WHEN I WALK THROUGH THE DARKEST
VALLEY, I WILL NOT BE AFRAID, FOR YOU ARE
CLOSE BESIDE ME. YOUR ROD AND YOUR STAFF
PROTECT AND COMFORT ME. *Psalm 23:4*

Desires

MY QUESTIONS *for* GOD

Is it wrong to have certain desires? How can I keep my desires in check?

A MOMENT *with* GOD

Hope deferred makes the heart sick, but a dream fulfilled is a tree of life.   PROVERBS 13:12

LORD, we show our trust in you by obeying your laws; our heart's desire is to glorify your name.

ISAIAH 26:8

Wherever your treasure is, there the desires of your heart will also be.   MATTHEW 6:21

God created you with a capacity to desire. Desire can be healthy or unhealthy, godly or ungodly, casual or intense. You can desire something simple, like a home-cooked meal, or you can develop a burning passion for a cause that eventually consumes you. Some desires fuel passions to white heat, even driving a person to violence and crime to satisfy those desires. Desire is good and healthy if it is directed toward the proper object: that which is good and right and God-honoring. The same basic desire can also be right or wrong, depending on your motives and the object of your desire. The desire to love someone, if directed toward your spouse, is healthy and right. But that same desire directed toward someone who is not your spouse is adultery. The desire to lead an organization is healthy if your motive is to serve others, but it is unhealthy and wrong if your motive is to gain the power to control others. The best way to develop healthy desires is to know God—to hunger and thirst for him. When you know him personally and come to love him deeply, he will help you control your other desires, tame them, and direct them down the path that honors him.

DIVINE PROMISE

GOD IS WORKING IN YOU, GIVING YOU THE DESIRE AND THE POWER TO DO WHAT PLEASES HIM. *Philippians 2:13*

Destiny

MY QUESTION *for* GOD

Do I really have a "destiny"?

A MOMENT *with* GOD

Whether we are here in this body or away from this body, our goal is to please him. For we must all stand before Christ to be judged. We will each receive whatever we deserve for the good or evil we have done in this earthly body.   2 CORINTHIANS 5:9-10

Seek the Kingdom of God above all else, and live righteously, and he will give you everything you need.   MATTHEW 6:33

My sheep listen to my voice; I know them, and they follow me. I give them eternal life, and they will never perish. No one can snatch them away from me, for my Father has given them to me, and he is more powerful than anyone else. No one can snatch them from the Father's hand.   JOHN 10:27-29

*K*nowing you will one day live with God in his eternal Kingdom helps you set your priorities on eternal needs rather than on worldly desires. It is your destiny to share with God in all the wonders and comforts of his Kingdom. When you pursue this destiny and embrace it with all you have, you will be pure of heart, enjoying each day in the sustaining love of God. You can live your life to the fullest with absolute confidence that death is not the end but only the beginning of life! This confidence gives you meaning and hope as you persevere through the troubles of this life.

DIVINE PROMISE

YOU WILL GUIDE ME WITH YOUR COUNSEL, LEADING ME TO A GLORIOUS DESTINY.   *Psalm 73:24*

Differences

MY QUESTION *for* GOD

What is the proper perspective on my differences with others?

A MOMENT *with* GOD

I appeal to you, dear brothers and sisters, by the
authority of our Lord Jesus Christ, to live in harmony
with each other. Let there be no divisions in the
church. Rather, be of one mind, united in thought
and purpose.   1 CORINTHIANS 1:10

Just as our bodies have many parts and each part has
a special function, so it is with Christ's body. We are
many parts of one body, and we all belong to each
other.   ROMANS 12:4-5

*J*ust as all kinds of instruments strengthen an or-
chestra, so people with different gifts and perspectives
make any team stronger. Too often we let differences
cause confusion, conflict, and tension. But God often
puts very different people together so that their gifts
can complement each other. It is often through such
diversity that the most progress is made. Your life,
your relationships, and your spiritual life all become
stagnant when you ignore or detest the differences of
others. But you will thrive in the beauty of progress
when you embrace the others' differences.

DIVINE PROMISE

ENCOURAGE EACH OTHER. LIVE IN HARMONY
AND PEACE. THEN THE GOD OF LOVE AND
PEACE WILL BE WITH YOU.   *2 Corinthians 13:11*

Disappointment

My Question *for* God

How can I handle life's disappointments?

A Moment *with* God

Dear friends, don't be surprised at the fiery trials
you are going through, as if something strange were
happening to you.   1 PETER 4:12

A man planted a fig tree in his garden and came
again and again to see if there was any fruit on it, but
he was always disappointed. Finally, he said to his
gardener, "I've waited three years, and there hasn't
been a single fig! Cut it down. It's just taking up
space in the garden."   LUKE 13:6-7

Always continue to fear the LORD. You will be
rewarded for this; your hope will not be disappointed.
                                                     PROVERBS 23:17-18

*D*isappointment in some form may haunt you almost
every day. Perhaps you didn't get everything done;
someone hurt you or let you down; you let someone
else down, or things didn't go your way. You may
have experienced that awful feeling of "not being good
enough." When facing disappointment, you might condemn yourself, ask the "what if" questions or focus on
"if only" statements that lead to regret. You might play
the blame game so that someone else is at fault. None
of these responses are appropriate, and all of them can

quickly lead to discouragement, depression, anger,
shame, or bitterness. When disappointment dominates
your thoughts, you can easily become a negative, sad,
grumpy person. But if you see disappointment as an opportunity to learn and grow, or if you choose to focus
on what you have and not on what you missed, then you
can put disappointment into perspective. Life is full of
disappointment. But God doesn't want you to dwell on
what could have been; he wants you to focus on what
can be. He is the God of hope who gives you the gift
of his approval. The next time you feel disappointed,
remember all you have, determine to use the time to
grow, and be happy that you have the approval of the
One who really matters.

DIVINE PROMISE

THIS HOPE WILL NOT LEAD TO
DISAPPOINTMENT. FOR WE KNOW HOW
DEARLY GOD LOVES US, BECAUSE HE HAS
GIVEN US THE HOLY SPIRIT TO FILL OUR
HEARTS WITH HIS LOVE.   *Romans 5:5*

Disaster

MY QUESTIONS *for* GOD

*Why does God allow disasters to happen? Why doesn't he
prevent them?*

A Moment *with* God

Your Father in heaven . . . sends rain on the just and
the unjust alike. MATTHEW 5:45

By means of their suffering, he rescues those who
suffer. For he gets their attention through adversity.
JOB 36:15

As surely as the LORD your God has given you the
good things he promised, he will also bring disaster
on you if you disobey him. JOSHUA 23:15

We know that God causes everything to work
together for the good of those who love God and are
called according to his purpose for them. ROMANS 8:28

For reasons only God knows, he allows disasters
to happen, not only to the ungodly but also to godly
people. He may allow a disaster in your life in order
to get your attention and to draw you back to himself.
Sometimes a disaster can be the result of sin. It can be
a consequence of your own sin or the ripple effect of
someone else's disobedience to God. Sometimes disaster is man-made, like war, and other times it comes
through nature in the form of a violent storm, a flood,
a fire or a drought. No matter what kind of disaster you
face, true faith believes that God still loves you and has
your best interests at heart. If you have experienced disaster, take the opportunity to learn as much as you can
about both God and yourself. And remember that God
himself is always with you in the midst of disaster.

DIVINE PROMISE

THE LORD HIMSELF, THE KING OF ISRAEL, WILL
LIVE AMONG YOU! AT LAST YOUR TROUBLES
WILL BE OVER, AND YOU WILL NEVER AGAIN
FEAR DISASTER.   *Zephaniah 3:15*

Discernment

MY QUESTION *for* GOD

Why should I strive for discernment?

A MOMENT *with* GOD

Solid food is for those who are mature, who through
training have the skill to recognize the difference
between right and wrong.   HEBREWS 5:14

I am writing to you not because you don't know the
truth but because you know the difference between
truth and lies.   1 JOHN 2:21

Give me understanding and I will obey your
instructions; I will put them into practice with all
my heart.   PSALM 119:34

Job said, "The ear tests the words it hears just as the
mouth distinguishes between foods." So let us discern
for ourselves what is right; let us learn together what
is good.   JOB 34:3-4

*D*iscernment is the ability to differentiate between right and wrong, true and false, good and bad, important and trivial, godly and ungodly. Discernment helps you properly interpret issues and understand the motives of those pushing a certain agenda. Discernment shows you the way through the maze of options that you face. Like the sun that burns away the fog, discernment cuts through confusion and distractions and brings clarity to life and its issues.

DIVINE PROMISE

LET THOSE WHO ARE WISE UNDERSTAND THESE THINGS. LET THOSE WITH DISCERNMENT LISTEN CAREFULLY. THE PATHS OF THE LORD ARE TRUE AND RIGHT, AND RIGHTEOUS PEOPLE LIVE BY WALKING IN THEM. BUT IN THOSE PATHS SINNERS STUMBLE AND FALL.   *Hosea 14:9*

Discipline

MY QUESTION *for* GOD

What is the purpose of discipline?

A MOMENT *with* GOD

Think about it: Just as a parent disciplines a child, the LORD your God disciplines you for your own good.

DEUTERONOMY 8:5

Joyful are those you discipline, LORD, those you teach with your instructions.   PSALM 94:12

As you endure this divine discipline, remember that
God is treating you as his own children.   Hebrews 12:7

The goal of discipline is to prevent you from harming
yourself and others, to build good character and habits,
and to teach you right from wrong. Undisciplined and
reckless actions are selfish and can damage your relationship with God and with others. God's discipline is
an act of love to keep you from damaging your most
important relationships and to help you become the
person God created you to be. He wants to prevent
your becoming an immature, selfish person. Left to
yourself, you will always tend to move away from God
and toward sin. God's discipline reminds you why obedience to him is best.

Divine Promise

NO DISCIPLINE IS ENJOYABLE WHILE IT IS
HAPPENING—IT'S PAINFUL! BUT AFTERWARD
THERE WILL BE A PEACEFUL HARVEST OF RIGHT
LIVING FOR THOSE WHO ARE TRAINED IN
THIS WAY.   *Hebrews 12:11*

Discontent

My Question *for* God

Why are so many people discontented when they have so much?

A Moment *with* God

The people complained and turned against Moses.
"What are we going to drink?" they demanded.

EXODUS 15:24

There, too, the whole community of Israel complained
about Moses and Aaron. "If only the LORD had killed
us back in Egypt," they moaned. "There we sat around
pots filled with meat and ate all the bread we wanted.
But now you have brought us into this wilderness to
starve us all to death."   EXODUS 16:2-3

When it was time for the harvest, Cain presented
some of his crops as a gift to the LORD. Abel also
brought a gift—the best of the firstborn lambs from
his flock. The LORD accepted Abel and his gift, but
he did not accept Cain and his gift. This made Cain
very angry, and he looked dejected. "Why are you
so angry?" the LORD asked Cain. "Why do you look
so dejected?"   GENESIS 4:3-6

True godliness with contentment is itself great
wealth. After all, we brought nothing with us when
we came into the world, and we can't take anything
with us when we leave it. So if we have enough food
and clothing, let us be content.   1 TIMOTHY 6:6-8

*D*iscontent sneaks into your life for a variety of reasons. Maybe you have allowed your present troubles
to overshadow the past blessings of God in your life.
Conversely, perhaps you are dwelling in the past and
missing out on the blessings of today. Your discontent

may come from confusing your wants with your needs and from comparing yourself to others and their possessions. In any case, discontent robs you of the joys in life and in your relationships with others and with God. To combat discontent, keep your focus on God; discipline your mind to find the good in every situation and to be thankful for your blessings.

DIVINE PROMISE

EVEN THOUGH THE FIG TREES HAVE NO BLOSSOMS, AND THERE ARE NO GRAPES ON THE VINES; EVEN THOUGH THE OLIVE CROP FAILS, AND THE FIELDS LIE EMPTY AND BARREN; EVEN THOUGH THE FLOCKS DIE IN THE FIELDS, AND THE CATTLE BARNS ARE EMPTY, YET I WILL REJOICE IN THE LORD! I WILL BE JOYFUL IN THE GOD OF MY SALVATION! THE SOVEREIGN LORD IS MY STRENGTH! HE MAKES ME AS SUREFOOTED AS A DEER, ABLE TO TREAD UPON THE HEIGHTS.   *Habakkuk 3:17-19*

Discovery

MY QUESTION *for* GOD

How can I discover God?

A MOMENT *with* GOD

I will pursue your commands, for you expand my understanding.   PSALM 119:32

My child, listen to what I say, and treasure my commands. Tune your ears to wisdom, and concentrate on understanding. Cry out for insight, and ask for understanding. Search for them as you would for silver; seek them like hidden treasures. Then you will understand what it means to fear the LORD, and you will gain knowledge of God.

PROVERBS 2:1-5

The word of God is alive and powerful.   HEBREWS 4:12

*O*ne of the best ways to discover God is to read his Word, the Bible, on a daily basis. It is filled with accounts of God's actions throughout history, his concern for individuals and groups of people, his plans for creation, his promises, and his commands. Throughout the Bible God reveals his character, unveils his redemptive plan, and brings truth into the light. There's no limit to your discoveries about God as you read his living and powerful words. The more you come to know him, the more you will want to know.

DIVINE PROMISE

I WILL GIVE YOU TREASURES HIDDEN IN THE DARKNESS—SECRET RICHES. I WILL DO THIS SO YOU MAY KNOW THAT I AM THE LORD, THE GOD OF ISRAEL, THE ONE WHO CALLS YOU BY NAME. *Isaiah 45:3*

Distractions

How can I handle all the distractions in my life?

A MOMENT *with* GOD

One day some parents brought their children to Jesus
so he could lay his hands on them and pray for them.
But the disciples scolded the parents for bothering
him. But Jesus said, "Let the children come to me.
Don't stop them! For the Kingdom of Heaven belongs
to those who are like these children." And he placed
his hands on their heads and blessed them before
he left.   MATTHEW 19:13-15

As Jesus was starting out on his way to Jerusalem,
a man came running up to him, knelt down, and
asked, "Good Teacher, what must I do to inherit
eternal life?"   MARK 10:17

Distractions bombarded Jesus all the time. But he
didn't see all of them as distractions; he saw some
as opportunities to save the lost or to help someone.
When someone needs you, a distraction can become
a divine opportunity to show them the love and care
of God. Sometimes God interrupts you for a good reason. Don't miss the chance to focus on the people God
brings to you for help.

DIVINE CHALLENGE

MARK OUT A STRAIGHT PATH FOR YOUR FEET
SO THAT THOSE WHO ARE WEAK AND LAME
WILL NOT FALL BUT BECOME STRONG.

Hebrews 12:13

Diversity

MY QUESTION *for* GOD

How is unity possible when we're all so different?

A MOMENT *with* GOD

There are different kinds of spiritual gifts, but the
same Spirit is the source of them all. There are
different kinds of service, but we serve the same
Lord. . . . The human body has many parts, but the
many parts make up one whole body. So it is with the
body of Christ. . . . But our bodies have many parts,
and God has put each part just where he wants it.

1 CORINTHIANS 12:4-5, 12, 18

Just as our bodies have many parts and each part has
a special function, so it is with Christ's body. We are
many parts of one body, and we all belong to each
other. In his grace, God has given us different gifts
for doing certain things well. So if God has given you
the ability to prophesy, speak out with as much faith
as God has given you.   ROMANS 12:4-6

The rich and poor have this in common: The LORD
made them both.   PROVERBS 22:2

*D*iversity is everywhere—in government, neighborhoods, business, and families. People are diverse in skin color, nationality, religion, looks, skills, abilities, interests, personalities. Our differences cause us to work well together as a team. They take pressure off us to be responsible for everything. Maybe most important, our differences demonstrate God's creativity in making us. He didn't want us all to be the same. Too often, diversity causes prejudice and hatred; we tend to be more comfortable when the people around us are just like us. But the Bible tells us to celebrate and embrace diversity because God created us to be different in order to accomplish the varieties of work that need to be done.

DIVINE PROMISE

THERE IS NO LONGER JEW OR GENTILE, SLAVE OR FREE, MALE AND FEMALE. FOR YOU ARE ALL ONE IN CHRIST JESUS. *Galatians 3:28*

Doubt

MY QUESTION *for* GOD

When I'm struggling and have doubts about God, does it mean my faith isn't real?

A MOMENT *with* GOD

Abram replied, "O Sovereign LORD, how can I be sure?"   GENESIS 15:8

John the Baptist . . . sent his disciples to ask Jesus, "Are you the Messiah we've been expecting, or should we keep looking for someone else?"

MATTHEW 11:2-3

Jesus told him, "You believe because you have seen me. Blessed are those who believe without seeing me."

JOHN 20:29

*M*any people in the Bible who are considered "pillars of faith" had moments of doubt. This doesn't mean they had little or no faith but rather that their faith was being challenged in a new way. When you have moments of doubt, you are probably in new territory. Don't let your doubt drive you away from God. Instead, use your doubt as a moment to begin a new conversation with God. He welcomes your doubts as an opportunity to give you new insights about his love for you and about how you can better relate to him and trust him more. As your doubts cause you to reach for him, you will find he is there, just as he has always been.

DIVINE PROMISE

GOD HAS SAID, "I WILL NEVER FAIL YOU. I WILL NEVER ABANDON YOU." *Hebrews 13:5*

Dreams

MY QUESTION *for* GOD

How can I know if a dream is from God?

A MOMENT *with* GOD

Never stop praying.   1 THESSALONIANS 5:17

I have heard these prophets say, "Listen to the dream
I had from God last night." And then they proceed to
tell lies in my name. How long will this go on? If they
are prophets, they are prophets of deceit, inventing
everything they say. By telling these false dreams,
they are trying to get my people to forget me. . . .
But let my true messengers faithfully proclaim my
every word. There is a difference between straw
and grain!   JEREMIAH 23:25-28

He asked the LORD what he should do, but the LORD
refused to answer him, either by dreams or by sacred
lots or by the prophets.   1 SAMUEL 28:6

God speaks to you in a variety of ways: through his
Word, through the wisdom of other godly people,
through nature, through your conscience, and sometimes through dreams and visions. If God speaks to
you in a dream, his message will always be consistent
with what he has already told you in his Word. He will
never contradict his own commandments or ask you to
do something immoral or illegal. If a dream moves you

to serve God with greater passion, do so; it may be God speaking to you in a new way!

DIVINE PROMISE

LONG AGO GOD SPOKE MANY TIMES AND IN MANY WAYS TO OUR ANCESTORS THROUGH THE PROPHETS. AND NOW IN THESE FINAL DAYS, HE HAS SPOKEN TO US THROUGH HIS SON.   *Hebrews 1:1-2*

Emotions

MY QUESTION *for* GOD

How can I best handle my emotions?

A MOMENT *with* GOD

Guard your heart above all else, for it determines the course of your life.   PROVERBS 4:23

I will give you a new heart, and I will put a new spirit in you. I will take out your stony, stubborn heart and give you a tender, responsive heart.   EZEKIEL 36:26

*Y*our emotions are a product of both your mind and your heart. The Bible says, "The human heart is the most deceitful of all things, and desperately wicked" (Jeremiah 17:9). It is the center of your emotions because it is where good and evil battle for control. Your emotions are greatly influenced by both the good and evil desires in your heart. It is wise to exercise caution when trusting your emotions, because evil desires pretending to be right desires can easily influence your feelings. The best way to handle your emotions is to guard your heart by controlling what you let in and out. It is not enough to merely abstain from letting poor influences into your mind and heart. You must also fill your heart with right desires from God's Word, which comes from God's own heart. As you become more in tune with God's heart, your own emotions will be more trustworthy and under control.

DIVINE PROMISE

THE HOLY SPIRIT PRODUCES THIS KIND
OF FRUIT IN OUR LIVES: LOVE, JOY,
PEACE, PATIENCE, KINDNESS, GOODNESS,
FAITHFULNESS, GENTLENESS, AND
SELF-CONTROL.   *Galatians 5:22-23*

Emptiness

MY QUESTION *for* GOD

I have so much, but I still feel empty inside. Where can I find fulfillment?

A MOMENT *with* GOD

Don't be dismayed when the wicked grow rich and their homes become ever more splendid. For when

they die, they take nothing with them. Their wealth
will not follow them into the grave.   PSALM 49:16-17

Riches won't help on the day of judgment, but right
living can save you from death.   PROVERBS 11:4

Enjoy what you have rather than desiring what
you don't have. Just dreaming about nice things is
meaningless—like chasing the wind.   ECCLESIASTES 6:9

May you experience the love of Christ, though it is
too great to understand fully. Then you will be made
complete with all the fullness of life and power that
comes from God.   EPHESIANS 3:19

Why do some foods satisfy your hunger for a long
time, while other foods fill you up for only a short
time? Material things are like the foods that just don't
fill you up for long. They can fill physical space, but
they can't fill space in your soul, and only when your
soul is filled will you be truly and deeply satisfied. Feelings of emptiness come when you try to fill yourself
with the wrong things, because eventually you realize
they don't satisfy you the way you thought they would.
That is because real fulfillment comes through relationship with God. The more you get to know God,
the more he pours his presence into your life and fills
you with blessings that satisfy—blessings such as love,
help, encouragement, peace, and comfort. These are
blessings of eternal satisfaction because they were created by God to last forever. If you are not filled with
God's Spirit and the blessings that come with it, then

your heart is like an empty home, waiting to be occu-
pied. When God comes into your life, you will find
true satisfaction and fulfillment.

DIVINE CHALLENGE

DON'T BE SO CONCERNED ABOUT PERISHABLE
THINGS LIKE FOOD. SPEND YOUR ENERGY
SEEKING THE ETERNAL LIFE THAT THE SON OF
MAN CAN GIVE YOU. FOR GOD THE FATHER
HAS GIVEN ME THE SEAL OF HIS APPROVAL.

John 6:27

Encouragement

MY QUESTION *for* GOD

How does God encourage me?

A MOMENT *with* GOD

Your Father knows exactly what you need even before
you ask him!   MATTHEW 6:8

Jesus turned around, and when he saw her he said,
"Daughter, be encouraged! Your faith has made you
well." And the woman was healed at that moment.

MATTHEW 9:22

May our Lord Jesus Christ himself and God our
Father, who loved us and by his grace gave us eternal
comfort and a wonderful hope, comfort you and
strengthen you in every good thing you do and say.

2 THESSALONIANS 2:16-17

*L*ife can be so discouraging at times. When your world seems to be crashing down around you and nothing is going well, it's comforting to know that your heavenly Father already knows exactly what you need! He knows if your discouragement is from physical weariness, emotional strain, mental taxation, relational strife, or spiritual apathy, and he is ready to meet you at your point of need. He will encourage you through his Word with comfort, hope and strength. Turn to him every day, and bask in his love.

DIVINE PROMISE

THE MORE WE SUFFER FOR CHRIST, THE MORE GOD WILL SHOWER US WITH HIS COMFORT THROUGH CHRIST. *2 Corinthians 1:5*

Endurance

MY QUESTION *for* GOD

Where do I find the endurance to keep going when I'm tempted to give up?

A MOMENT *with* GOD

I am certain that God, who began the good work within you, will continue his work until it is finally finished on the day when Christ Jesus returns.

PHILIPPIANS 1:6

When troubles come your way, consider it an opportunity for great joy. For you know that when your faith is tested, your endurance has a chance to grow. So let it grow, for when your endurance is fully developed, you will be perfect and complete, needing nothing.   JAMES 1:2-4

These trials will show that your faith is genuine. It is being tested as fire tests and purifies gold—though your faith is far more precious than mere gold. So when your faith remains strong through many trials, it will bring you much praise and glory and honor on the day when Jesus Christ is revealed to the whole world.   1 PETER 1:7

*Y*ou don't have to depend only on your own strength to endure. God offers to help you, giving you strength and his supernatural power to sustain you. He gives you the strength to keep going when you are exhausted and the faith to keep believing when you are discouraged. Endurance is like the fire that purifies precious metals and hardens valuable pottery. It cleanses, clarifies, and solidifies your faith. Living through the trials and tests of life is often the most significant way to discover the riches of your faith and develop godly character.

DIVINE PROMISE

HE WILL GIVE ETERNAL LIFE TO THOSE WHO KEEP ON DOING GOOD, SEEKING AFTER THE GLORY AND HONOR AND IMMORTALITY THAT GOD OFFERS. *Romans 2:7*

Enemies

MY QUESTION *for* GOD

How can my enemies defeat me?

A MOMENT *with* GOD

Delilah pouted, "How can you tell me, 'I love you,'
when you don't share your secrets with me?" . . . She
tormented him with her nagging day after day until
he was sick to death of it. Finally, Samson shared his
secret with her. . . . So the Philistines captured him
and . . . he was bound with bronze chains.

JUDGES 16:15-17, 21

Do not let sin control the way you live; do not give in
to sinful desires.   ROMANS 6:12

Dear friend, don't let this bad example influence you.
Follow only what is good.   3 JOHN 1:11

The crafty Philistines knew they couldn't match
Samson's brute strength, so they aimed at his weakness—his inability to stay away from seductive women.
Temptation always strikes at your weak spot. "How can
you say you love me?" Delilah whined—and Samson
gave in. Your weak spots are those areas that you refuse
to give over to God. They are joints in your spiritual
armor at which the enemy takes aim, the areas in which
you compromise your convictions for a few moments
of pleasure. It is those areas of weakness where you
must ask God for the most help so he can cover your

vulnerable spots with his strength. You must understand your weaknesses so you can arm yourself against
Satan's attacks. It is a disaster to discover your weak
spots in the heat of the battle, as Samson did; you must
discover them before the fighting begins. With a strat-
egy to protect your points of vulnerability, you will be
prepared for the enemy's attacks.

DIVINE PROMISE

BE STRONG IN THE LORD AND IN HIS MIGHTY
POWER. PUT ON ALL OF GOD'S ARMOR SO THAT
YOU WILL BE ABLE TO STAND FIRM AGAINST ALL
STRATEGIES OF THE DEVIL.   *Ephesians 6:10-11*

Eternity

MY QUESTION *for* GOD

*Eternal life with God sounds kind of boring. Why should I
look forward to living with him forever?*

A MOMENT *with* GOD

God has made everything beautiful for its own time.
He has planted eternity in the human heart, but even
so, people cannot see the whole scope of God's work
from beginning to end.   ECCLESIASTES 3:11

No eye has seen, no ear has heard, and no mind
has imagined what God has prepared for those who
love him.   1 CORINTHIANS 2:9

$\mathcal{K}$ing Solomon wrote in the book of Ecclesiastes that God has planted eternity in the human heart (Ecclesiastes 3:11). This means that you innately know there is more than just this life. Something you were made for is still missing. Because you are created in God's image, you have eternal value, and nothing but the eternal God can truly satisfy. He has built into you a restless yearning for the kind of perfect world that can be found only in heaven. Through nature, art, and relationships he gives you a glimpse of that world. Someday he will restore earth to the way it was when he first created it, when it was perfect, and eternity will be a never-ending exploration of its beauty and a perfect relationship with God.

DIVINE PROMISE

DON'T LET YOUR HEARTS BE TROUBLED. TRUST IN GOD, AND TRUST ALSO IN ME. THERE IS MORE THAN ENOUGH ROOM IN MY FATHER'S HOME. IF THIS WERE NOT SO, WOULD I HAVE TOLD YOU THAT I AM GOING TO PREPARE A PLACE FOR YOU? WHEN EVERYTHING IS READY, I WILL COME AND GET YOU, SO THAT YOU WILL ALWAYS BE WITH ME WHERE I AM.   *John 14:1-3*

$\mathcal{E}$xcellence

MY QUESTIONS *for* GOD

Why does God encourage excellence? Why should I strive to be excellent?

A MOMENT *with* GOD

The LORD has filled Bezalel with the Spirit of God,
giving him great wisdom, ability, and expertise in all
kinds of crafts. He is a master craftsman, expert in
working with gold, silver, and bronze. He is skilled
in engraving and mounting gemstones and in carving
wood. He is a master at every craft. And the LORD
has given both him and Oholiab son of Ahisamach,
of the tribe of Dan, the ability to teach their skills
to others. The LORD has given them special skills as
engravers, designers, embroiderers in blue, purple,
and scarlet thread on fine linen cloth, and weavers.
They excel as craftsmen and as designers.

EXODUS 35:31-35

*E*xcellence is not better mediocrity; it is not more of
the same old thing. Rather, it is a new and higher standard. You not only admire and appreciate the charac-
teristics that bring about excellence (hard work, skill,
persistence, vision, knowledge, caring), but you also
admire and appreciate the end result of excellence
(beauty, quality, functionality, victory, teamwork, inspiration). God places great value on excellence and
therefore created you with unique and special gifts to
help you become especially excellent in some area.

God looked over all he had made, and he saw that it
was very good!   GENESIS 1:31

Do you have the gift of helping others? Do it with all
the strength and energy that God supplies.   1 PETER 4:11

Imitate God, therefore, in everything you do, because
you are his dear children.   EPHESIANS 5:1

*Y*our pursuit of excellence helps others experience
excellence, giving them a glimpse of God and inspiring
them to pursue excellence themselves. God initiated
excellence in the beauty of his creation, and you are
called to perpetuate it. You do this first by striving to
accomplish God's purpose in your life to the best of
your ability. Your life speaks of excellence when you
consistently strive to model yourself after God's perfect character as you go about the work he has called
you to do. You'll never be perfect in this life, but as
you work toward that goal, you will model excellence
to those around you.

DIVINE PROMISE

WORK WILLINGLY AT WHATEVER YOU DO, AS
THOUGH YOU WERE WORKING FOR THE LORD
RATHER THAN FOR PEOPLE. REMEMBER THAT
THE LORD WILL GIVE YOU AN INHERITANCE AS
YOUR REWARD, AND THAT THE MASTER YOU
ARE SERVING IS CHRIST. *Colossians 3:23-24*

Experience

MY QUESTION *for* GOD

How can I truly experience God?

A MOMENT *with* GOD

God blesses those whose hearts are pure, for they
will see God.   MATTHEW 5:8

We can be sure that we know [God] if we obey his
commandments.   1 JOHN 2:3

God is working in you, giving you the desire and the
power to do what pleases him.   PHILIPPIANS 2:13

A pure heart with steady obedience to God's commands makes your heart ripe to experience God's
work in you. As his Spirit within you instructs and inspires your obedience to him, you come to know him
by knowing his ways. The more you obey, the more
you will recognize and experience the work of God's
Spirit within you encouraging you, empowering you,
and guiding you in God's ways. Then you will come to
know God and see how he has touched your life.

DIVINE PROMISE

MAY YOU EXPERIENCE THE LOVE OF CHRIST,
THOUGH IT IS TOO GREAT TO UNDERSTAND
FULLY. THEN YOU WILL BE MADE COMPLETE
WITH ALL THE FULLNESS OF LIFE AND POWER
THAT COMES FROM GOD.   *Ephesians 3:19*

Failure

MY QUESTION *for* GOD

How can God bring anything good from my failure?

A MOMENT *with* GOD

People who conceal their sins will not prosper,
but if they confess and turn from them, they will
receive mercy.   PROVERBS 28:13

Examine yourselves to see if your faith is genuine.
Test yourselves. Surely you know that Jesus Christ is
among you; if not, you have failed the test of genuine
faith.   2 CORINTHIANS 13:5

We know that God causes everything to work
together for the good of those who love God and are
called according to his purpose for them.   ROMANS 8:28

Failure presents an opportunity to examine yourself
and find your flaws. Rather than give up, you are wise
to ask God to use you *despite* your flaws. When you
have failed, it is a good time to restore your relationship with God by admitting your mistakes and asking
for forgiveness. God can use your humbled spirit and
brokenness to rebuild you into the person he created
you to be.

DIVINE PROMISE

THE LORD DIRECTS THE STEPS OF THE GODLY.
HE DELIGHTS IN EVERY DETAIL OF THEIR
LIVES. THOUGH THEY STUMBLE, THEY WILL
NEVER FALL, FOR THE LORD HOLDS THEM BY
THE HAND.   *Psalm 37:23-24*

Faith

MY QUESTION *for* GOD

How does faith in God affect how I live?

A MOMENT *with* GOD

I tell you the truth, those who listen to my message
and believe in God who sent me have eternal life.

JOHN 5:24

Faith is the confidence that what we hope for will
actually happen; it gives us assurance about things we
cannot see.   HEBREWS 11:1

Faith is more than just believing; it is trusting your
very life to what you believe. You can believe that
someone can walk across a deep gorge on a tightrope.
But are you willing to trust that person to carry you
across? Faith would say yes. Faith in God means that
you are willing to trust him to carry you across the
tightrope of life. You are willing to follow his guidelines for living as outlined in the Bible because you have
the conviction that this will be best for you. You are

even willing to endure ridicule and persecution for your faith because you are so sure that God is who he says he is and will keep his promises of salvation and eternal life in heaven.

DIVINE PROMISE

BELIEVE IN THE LORD JESUS AND YOU WILL BE SAVED. *Acts 16:31*

Faithfulness

MY QUESTION *for* GOD

How is God faithful to me?

A MOMENT *with* GOD

You can be sure of this: The LORD set apart the godly for himself. The LORD will answer when I call to him.

PSALM 4:3

Hear my prayer, O LORD; listen to my plea! Answer me because you are faithful and righteous.

PSALM 143:1

God . . . is faithful to do what he says, and he has invited you into partnership with his Son, Jesus Christ our Lord.

1 CORINTHIANS 1:9

$\mathcal{G}$od faithfully does what he says he will do. As you read the Bible, you will discover myriads of promises God has already fulfilled. When you read the promises yet to come, you can count on God's faithfulness to fulfill them because he always does just what he says. When you call on God, he faithfully answers. His answer isn't always what you want to hear, but it is always what is best for you. God always listens and responds to those he loves.

DIVINE PROMISE

SURELY YOUR GOODNESS AND UNFAILING
LOVE WILL PURSUE ME ALL THE DAYS OF
MY LIFE.   *Psalm 23:6*

$\mathcal{F}$asting

MY QUESTION *for* GOD

Why should I fast?

A MOMENT *with* GOD

When this vision came to me, I, Daniel, had been in mourning for three whole weeks. All that time I had eaten no rich food. No meat or wine crossed my lips, and I used no fragrant lotions until those three weeks had passed.   DANIEL 10:2-3

I turned to the LORD God and pleaded with him
in prayer and fasting. I also wore rough burlap and
sprinkled myself with ashes.   DANIEL 9:3

$\mathscr{S}$ometimes the routine of life can inhibit communication with God. Therefore, it may at times be necessary
and healthy to abstain from certain things that are a
part of your daily routine. Fasting is the act of abstain-
ing from or limiting food in order to more fully focus
on God. It tells God that you are serious about com-
muning with him. Fasting sharpens your mind, allow-
ing you to be more receptive to what God has to say.
Sometimes you can do a full fast, but sometimes a par-
tial fast is all you can do, giving up only some foods. At
times you may sense the need to support your prayers
and spiritual activities with fasting and yet sustain your
health and energy. In such times you may give up significant items, as Daniel gave up rich foods. Fasting
is about communication with God. Think about how
much time you spend thinking about, preparing, and
enjoying your meals. What if every once in a while you
eliminated that part of your routine in order to allow
more time for God to break through in your life?

DIVINE PROMISE

WHEN YOU FAST, DON'T MAKE IT OBVIOUS. . . .
THEN NO ONE WILL NOTICE THAT YOU ARE
FASTING, EXCEPT YOUR FATHER, WHO KNOWS
WHAT YOU DO IN PRIVATE. AND YOUR FATHER,
WHO SEES EVERYTHING, WILL REWARD YOU.
Matthew 6:16-18

Fear

MY QUESTION *for* GOD

What does it mean to fear God?

A MOMENT *with* GOD

Doesn't his majesty terrify you? Doesn't your fear of
him overwhelm you?   JOB 13:11

Let the whole world fear the LORD, and let everyone
stand in awe of him.   PSALM 33:8

How joyful are those who fear the LORD—all who
follow his ways!   PSALM 128:1

Fear of the LORD is the foundation of wisdom.
Knowledge of the Holy One results in good
judgment.   PROVERBS 9:10

Fearing God is not the same as being afraid of God.
Being afraid of someone drives you away from that
person. Fearing God means being awed by his power
and goodness. This draws you closer to him and to the
blessings he gives. When you fear God, it is similar to
the respect you have for a beloved teacher, coach, parent, or mentor who motivates you to do your best and
avoid doing anything that would offend that person or
provoke his or her displeasure. You fear God because
of his awesome power; you love God for the way he
blesses you with it.

Serve the LORD with reverent fear, and rejoice with
trembling.   PSALM 2:11

$\mathscr{B}$ecause God is so great and mighty, and because he holds the power of life and death in his hands, you should have a reverent awe of him. A healthy fear of God recognizes what he could do if he gave you what you deserved. But God is even more awesome because instead, he gives you mercy and forgiveness. A healthy fear should drive you to God for forgiveness and inspire gratitude for his love.

DIVINE PROMISE

DON'T BE AFRAID, FOR I AM WITH YOU.
DON'T BE DISCOURAGED, FOR I AM YOUR GOD.
I WILL STRENGTHEN YOU AND HELP YOU.
I WILL HOLD YOU UP WITH MY VICTORIOUS
RIGHT HAND.   *Isaiah 41:10*

$\mathscr{F}inishing$

MY QUESTION *for* GOD

What can inspire me to finish well?

A MOMENT *with* GOD

The years passed, and the LORD had given the people of Israel rest from all their enemies. Joshua, who was now very old, called together all the elders, leaders, judges, and officers of Israel. He said to them, "I am now a very old man. You have seen everything the LORD your God has done for you during my lifetime. The LORD your God has fought for you against your

enemies. . . . So be very careful to follow everything
Moses wrote in the Book of Instruction. Do not
deviate from it, turning either to the right or to the
left. . . . Cling tightly to the LORD your God as you
have done until now.   JOSHUA 23:1-3, 6-8

As the years take a toll on our bodies, it is painful to
realize that we no longer possess the physical skills or
energy we used to have. As old age settles on us, the
wrinkles, aches, and pains make us realize that our
lives are nearing their final chapter. But one of the sad-
dest things is when older people are dismissed as if their
earthly contributions are finished. Joshua, as an old
man, demonstrated that older believers can be a powerful witness to the persistent mercy and faithfulness of
God. There are few things as powerful as the testimony
of one who has lived a long life of faithfulness to the
Lord and still maintains the vibrant vision of an eternal God who keeps his promises. Younger people who
listen to their life stories will be greatly influenced by
seeing God's faithfulness to them through the decades.
If you are a young person, find older believers and ask
them to tell you about God's faithfulness in their lives.
Be prepared to hear some amazing stories. If you are
older, commit yourself to finishing well. When you
demonstrate faithfulness to God to the end, your story
will become a divine moment in the lives of those who
come after you.

DIVINE PROMISE

I AM CERTAIN THAT GOD, WHO BEGAN THE
GOOD WORK WITHIN YOU, WILL CONTINUE
HIS WORK UNTIL IT IS FINALLY FINISHED ON
THE DAY WHEN CHRIST JESUS RETURNS.

Philippians 1:6

Putting Out a Fleece

MY QUESTION *for* GOD

What does it mean to "put out a fleece"?

A MOMENT *with* GOD

Gideon said to God, "If you are truly going to use
me to rescue Israel as you promised, prove it to me
in this way. I will put a wool fleece on the threshing
floor tonight. If the fleece is wet with dew in the
morning but the ground is dry, then I will know
that you are going to help me rescue Israel as you
promised."   JUDGES 6:36-37

The phrase *putting out a fleece* comes from the story
of Gideon in the Bible. It means that you designate a
sign that will confirm what you understand to be God's
will in a particular situation. How often in your prayers
do you tell God, "If only you would do this, then I
would know what to do"? A person must exercise great
caution when putting out a fleece, because doing so
tends to limit the options of a God who has unlimited

options available to you. It is also dangerous because of
the temptation to blame God if the decision doesn't go
the way you wanted. Don't try to force God to make a
decision from your limited range of options. Be willing
for him to work his way from his unlimited options.
When God has asked you to do something, show your
belief in him by taking him at his word and trusting
him to guide you into the next steps.

DIVINE PROMISE

IF YOU NEED WISDOM, ASK OUR GENEROUS
GOD, AND HE WILL GIVE IT TO YOU. HE WILL
NOT REBUKE YOU FOR ASKING.   *James 1:5*

Flexibility

MY QUESTION *for* GOD

*How does being flexible make me available for divine
moments with God?*

A MOMENT *with* GOD

We've given up everything to follow you.

MATTHEW 19:27

If any of you wants to be my follower, you must turn
from your selfish ways, take up your cross, and follow
me. If you try to hang on to your life, you will lose
it. But if you give up your life for my sake and for the
sake of the Good News, you will save it.   MARK 8:34-35

*B*eing flexible allows you to leave behind anything that might take your focus off God and to devote yourself to him with all your heart when he calls. This kind of availability to God prepares your heart for surprise moments with him as he guides you through life. God blesses you not because of your ability but because of your availability.

As soon as they landed, they left everything and followed Jesus.   LUKE 5:11

*F*lexibility understands the importance of God's timing and allows room in your life to change your plans. Flexibility means that no matter what you do, you can do it with an attitude of service to God. Flexibility develops through an eagerness to go where he calls you and serve where he shows you. It's a lifestyle change, now and forever.

DIVINE PROMISE

YOU MUST REMAIN FAITHFUL TO WHAT YOU HAVE BEEN TAUGHT FROM THE BEGINNING. IF YOU DO, YOU WILL REMAIN IN FELLOWSHIP WITH THE SON AND WITH THE FATHER. AND IN THIS FELLOWSHIP WE ENJOY THE ETERNAL LIFE HE PROMISED US. *1 John 2:24-25*

Following

MY QUESTION *for* GOD

Why does following God seem so hard sometimes?

A MOMENT *with* GOD

Jesus said to his disciples, "If any of you wants to be my follower, you must turn from your selfish ways, take up your cross, and follow me."   MATTHEW 16:24

Be strong and courageous, and do the work. Don't be afraid or discouraged, for the LORD God, my God, is with you. He will not fail you or forsake you.

1 CHRONICLES 28:20

*T*he fact that you are following God in a particular situation doesn't make it easy to do so. In fact, the more important a task is, the more evil forces will throw up roadblocks. If you know God is leading you in a certain direction, don't give up just because the going gets tough. If anything, that should tell you that you are headed in the right direction. Keep moving forward boldly with your eyes fixed on God. Your faith will be strengthened as you obey him in your life and in your daily choices, and when you do, you will be able to step out with stronger faith wherever God calls you.

DIVINE PROMISE

WHEN TROUBLES COME YOUR WAY, CONSIDER
IT AN OPPORTUNITY FOR GREAT JOY. FOR YOU
KNOW THAT WHEN YOUR FAITH IS TESTED,
YOUR ENDURANCE HAS A CHANCE TO GROW.
SO LET IT GROW, FOR WHEN YOUR ENDURANCE
IS FULLY DEVELOPED, YOU WILL BE PERFECT
AND COMPLETE, NEEDING NOTHING.   *James 1:2-4*

Forgiveness

MY QUESTIONS *for* GOD

*Will God forgive me for the things I've done wrong? Why
would he even want to forgive me?*

A MOMENT *with* GOD

I tell you the truth, all sin and blasphemy can be
forgiven.   MARK 3:28

Everyone who calls on the name of the LORD will
be saved.   JOEL 2:32

Nothing can ever separate us from God's love.

                                         ROMANS 8:38

He forgives all my sins and heals all my diseases.
. . . He does not punish us for all our sins; he does
not deal harshly with us, as we deserve. For his
unfailing love toward those who fear him is as great
as the height of the heavens above the earth. He has
removed our sins as far from us as the east is from
the west.   PSALM 103:3, 10-12

Forgiveness is not based on the magnitude of the sin but on the magnitude of the forgiver's love. Nothing you've done is so bad that God's complete and unconditional love can't forgive it. The Bible does, however, mention one unforgivable sin: harboring an attitude of defiant hostility toward God that prevents you from accepting his forgiveness. Only those who don't want his forgiveness are out of its reach. No matter how seriously you've messed up, it will never be enough for God to turn his back on you and deny you forgiveness when you ask him for it.

DIVINE PROMISE

"COME NOW, LET'S SETTLE THIS," SAYS THE LORD. "THOUGH YOUR SINS ARE LIKE SCARLET, I WILL MAKE THEM AS WHITE AS SNOW. THOUGH THEY ARE RED LIKE CRIMSON, I WILL MAKE THEM AS WHITE AS WOOL." *Isaiah 1:18*

Fun

MY QUESTION *for* GOD

Can I follow God and still have fun?

A MOMENT *with* GOD

For everything there is a season, a time for every activity under heaven. A time to . . . cry and a time to laugh. A time to grieve and a time to dance.

ECCLESIASTES 3:1-4

Go and celebrate with a feast . . . and share gifts of food with people who have nothing prepared. This is a sacred day. . . . Don't be . . . sad, for the joy of the LORD is your strength! NEHEMIAH 8:10

You have been faithful in handling this small amount. . . . Let's celebrate together! MATTHEW 25:21

The life of the godly is full of light and joy, but the light of the wicked will be snuffed out. PROVERBS 13:9

*J*udging from the number of feasts and festivals God instituted for the Israelites, he intended for his people to have times of fun. Following God doesn't exclude fun. Following God's commandments is the way to get the most out of life—to enjoy life as it was originally created to be enjoyed. God desires for you to have a rich life, to celebrate with others, and to find joy in your relationship with him. Joy, fun, and celebration as God intended are important parts of believing in God because they lift your spirits and help you see the beauty and meaning in life. These enjoyable experiences give you a small taste of the joy you will experience in heaven.

DIVINE PROMISE

THE GODLY CAN LOOK FORWARD TO A REWARD, WHILE THE WICKED CAN EXPECT ONLY JUDGMENT. *Proverbs 11:23*

Future

Can I really trust God with my future?

A MOMENT *with* GOD

The LORD says, "I will guide you along the best pathway for your life. I will advise you and watch over you."   PSALM 32:8

"I know the plans I have for you," says the LORD. "They are plans for good and not for disaster, to give you a future and a hope."   JEREMIAH 29:11

I am certain that God, who began the good work within you, will continue his work until it is finally finished on the day when Christ Jesus returns.

PHILIPPIANS 1:6

God directs your steps. He knows what you will encounter on the road of life, and only he can direct you in the best way for you to go. Although the path may lead through some dark valleys or seem to take some unnecessary detours, you will one day look back and discover that God's way really was best. God finishes what he starts. Don't allow your limitations or your present difficulties to blind you to the promise that God will complete his work in you. Your present insecurities are opportunities for God's work in your heart. As long as he has work for you, you can be sure God will guide you to where you need to be.

DIVINE PROMISE

YOU GUIDE ME WITH YOUR COUNSEL, LEADING
ME TO A GLORIOUS DESTINY. *Psalm 73:24*

Generosity

MY QUESTION *for* GOD

What does generosity look like?

A MOMENT *with* GOD

While Jesus was in the Temple, he watched the rich
people dropping their gifts in the collection box.
Then a poor widow came by and dropped in two
small coins. "I tell you the truth," Jesus said, "this
poor widow has given more than all the rest of them.
For they have given a tiny part of their surplus, but
she, poor as she is, has given everything she has."

LUKE 21:1-4

Wherever your treasure is, there the desires of your
heart will also be.   MATTHEW 6:21

Don't forget to do good and to share with those in
need. These are the sacrifices that please God.

HEBREWS 13:16

You must each decide in your heart how much to
give. And don't give reluctantly or in response
to pressure. "For God loves a person who gives
cheerfully."   2 CORINTHIANS 9:7

Who is more generous: a billionaire who gives one million dollars to his church, or a poor single mom who gives one hundred dollars? And if you have a lot of money, does that mean you are not generous? Jesus said you can't know the answer to those questions without knowing the heart of the giver. Throughout the Bible, God doesn't focus on how much money you have but rather on how generous you are with it. One thing is clear: Wherever your money goes reveals what you believe is most important. It's not what you have but what you do with what you have that is significant, whether it's money, time, or talents. Generosity is both a spiritual gift and a spiritual discipline. To some, generosity comes easily; others must work hard at it. But no one can afford to neglect it. Generosity is an important character trait to God because it is the opposite of selfishness, which along with pride, are two of the most destructive sins. Selfishness promotes greed, stinginess, envy, and hard-heartedness—traits that destroy relationships. Generosity promotes giving, trust, mercy, and putting others' needs above your own—traits that build relationships. And true generosity involves sacrifice, which is the key to changing your heart from stinginess to selflessness. Realizing that all you have is a gift from a generous God motivates you to share your material and earthly possessions more freely.

DIVINE PROMISE

REMEMBER THE WORDS OF THE LORD JESUS, "IT IS MORE BLESSED TO GIVE THAN TO RECEIVE."
Acts 20:35

Goals

MY QUESTION *for* GOD

Why are goals important?

A MOMENT *with* GOD

Look straight ahead, and fix your eyes on what lies before you. Mark out a straight path for your feet; stay on the safe path. Don't get sidetracked; keep your feet from following evil. PROVERBS 4:25-27

We are always confident, even though we know that as long as we live in these bodies we are not at home with the Lord. For we live by believing and not by seeing. . . . So whether we are here in this body or away from this body, our goal is to please him.

2 CORINTHIANS 5:6-9

All athletes are disciplined in their training. They do it to win a prize that will fade away, but we do it for an eternal prize. 1 CORINTHIANS 9:25

Setting goals is important if you want your life to count for anything. If you set no goals for getting anywhere in life, in the end, you will have achieved it—you will have gotten nowhere! It's good to set daily and short-term goals and equally important to set long-term goals. But have you thought about setting eternal goals? Do you spend more time planning for your retirement than for eternity? Ironically, it is planning for eternity that helps you prioritize your daily life.

DIVINE PROMISE

SEEK THE KINGDOM OF GOD ABOVE ALL ELSE,
AND LIVE RIGHTEOUSLY, AND HE WILL GIVE
YOU EVERYTHING YOU NEED.

Matthew 6:33

Goodness

MY QUESTION *for* GOD

How can I be a good person?

A MOMENT *with* GOD

[Jesus said,] "I tell you the truth, anyone who believes
in me will do the same works I have done." JOHN 14:12

All of us who have had that veil removed can see and
reflect the glory of the Lord. And the Lord—who is
the Spirit—makes us more and more like him as we
are changed into his glorious image.   2 CORINTHIANS 3:18

There once was a man named Job who lived in the
land of Uz. He was blameless—a man of complete
integrity. He feared God and stayed away from evil.

JOB 1:1

Goodness is not merely being good at something. It
is the by-product of a praiseworthy character. True
goodness runs deeper than nice actions; it reflects a
heart of integrity. If you want to be a good person, you
have to be willing for God to change you inside, deep

down in the inner core. As you become more and more like Jesus, your actions will reflect his goodness. As he takes control of your heart, you will begin doing good deeds, which when practiced over a lifetime, will be defined as goodness.

DIVINE PROMISE

THE LORD IS GOOD TO THOSE WHO DEPEND ON HIM, TO THOSE WHO SEARCH FOR HIM.
Lamentations 3:25

Grace

MY QUESTION *for* GOD

How does grace affect the way I live?

A MOMENT *with* GOD

God saved you by his grace when you believed. And you can't take credit for this; it is a gift from God. Salvation is not a reward for the good things we have done, so none of us can boast about it.

EPHESIANS 2:8-9

The wages of sin is death, but the free gift of God is eternal life through Christ Jesus our Lord.

ROMANS 6:23

Grace is like the gift of life itself: You can't take credit for it any more than a baby can brag about being born! The fact that grace is God's gift and not the product of your own effort gives you great comfort, security, and hope each day as you learn to live in the light of God's grace rather than in your own guilt. When you grasp the wonderful concept that God loves you and has broken the power of sin through Christ's death on the cross, you will be free to experience the transforming power of God's grace in your life.

DIVINE PROMISE

SIN IS NO LONGER YOUR MASTER, FOR YOU NO LONGER LIVE UNDER THE REQUIREMENTS OF THE LAW. INSTEAD, YOU LIVE UNDER THE FREEDOM OF GOD'S GRACE.   *Romans 6:14*

Grief

MY QUESTION *for* GOD

How should I respond when I'm hit with grief?

A MOMENT *with* GOD

The king was overcome with emotion. He went up to the room over the gateway and burst into tears. And as he went, he cried, "O my son Absalom! My son, my son Absalom! If only I had died instead of you! O Absalom, my son, my son."   2 SAMUEL 18:33

Joseph threw himself on his father and wept
over him.   GENESIS 50:1

I will comfort you there in Jerusalem as a mother
comforts her child.   ISAIAH 66:13

God is our merciful Father and the source of
all comfort.   2 CORINTHIANS 1:3

Grieving is necessary and important. You need the
time and the freedom to grieve. It is an important part
of healing because it allows you to release the emotional pressure of your sorrow. You can be strong
through your time of grief not by hiding it or acting
strong but by acknowledging your loss and expressing
it appropriately. God knows you grieve, understands
your sorrow, and comforts you with his presence. He
does not promise to protect you from grief, but he does
promise to help you through it. He has overcome all
things that cause grief, so take comfort in the knowledge that if you endure with God, you will overcome
with him.

DIVINE PROMISE

HE WILL WIPE EVERY TEAR FROM THEIR EYES,
AND THERE WILL BE NO MORE DEATH OR
SORROW OR CRYING OR PAIN. ALL THESE
THINGS ARE GONE FOREVER.

Revelation 21:4

Growth

How do I grow spiritually?

A MOMENT *with* GOD

Christ will make his home in your hearts as you trust in him. Your roots will grow down into God's love and keep you strong.   EPHESIANS 3:17

When I was a child, I spoke and thought and reasoned as a child. But when I grew up, I put away childish things.   1 CORINTHIANS 13:11

Let us stop going over the basic teachings about Christ again and again. Let us go on instead and become mature in our understanding.   HEBREWS 6:1

Spiritual growth is like physical growth: You start small and grow one day at a time. As you grow, however, you need nourishment. Spiritually you get this by challenging your mind to study God's Word, ask questions about it, and seek answers through prayer, the counsel of other believers, and life's experiences. Look at each day as a building block. When you commit to building a life of godly character one day at a time, you will find yourself growing more and more spiritually mature.

Divine Promise

WE ASK GOD TO GIVE YOU COMPLETE
KNOWLEDGE OF HIS WILL AND TO GIVE YOU
SPIRITUAL WISDOM AND UNDERSTANDING.
THEN THE WAY YOU LIVE WILL ALWAYS HONOR
AND PLEASE THE LORD, AND YOUR LIVES WILL
PRODUCE EVERY KIND OF GOOD FRUIT. ALL
THE WHILE, YOU WILL GROW AS YOU LEARN TO
KNOW GOD BETTER AND BETTER.   *Colossians 1:9-10*

Guidance

My Question *for* God

How can I experience God's guidance in my life?

A Moment *with* God

God's way is perfect. All the LORD's promises
prove true. He is a shield for all who look to him
for protection.   Psalm 18:30

The LORD directs the steps of the godly. He delights
in every detail of their lives.   Psalm 37:23

Trust in the LORD with all your heart; do not depend
on your own understanding. Seek his will in all you
do, and he will show you which path to take.

Proverbs 3:5-6

The first step is knowing where to put your trust.
Travelers rely on an accurate map when they don't

know where they are going. A critically ill person relies on medical experts who know the proper treatment. In the same way, believers realize their own spiritual limitations and rely on God's Word, which is life's instruction manual in matters of faith. You do not understand all the complexities of life, but God does. Trust him to guide you in finding and recognizing what is true.

The LORD says, "I will guide you along the best pathway for your life. I will advise you and watch over you."   PSALM 32:8

As you travel through life, it is important to have a close relationship with the ultimate guide—God. He knows where you've been and what will happen in the future. When you seek his guidance, he points you to places of unimaginable beauty, joy, and peace and also helps you avoid dangerous spots. God promises to be your constant guide in this journey called life. He will lead you through dark valleys and over mountaintop experiences and will bring you to that place of eternal peace and rest you long for.

DIVINE PROMISE

THAT IS WHAT GOD IS LIKE. HE IS OUR GOD FOREVER AND EVER, AND HE WILL GUIDE US UNTIL WE DIE.   *Psalm 48:14*

Habits

My Questions *for* God

Why do I always seem to develop bad habits, even when I feel in control? How can I break the cycle?

A Moment *with* God

Those who are dominated by the sinful nature think about sinful things, but those who are controlled by the Holy Spirit think about things that please the Spirit. So letting your sinful nature control your mind leads to death. But letting the Spirit control your mind leads to life and peace.   ROMANS 8:5-6

Do not let sin control the way you live; do not give in to sinful desires. Do not let any part of your body become an instrument of evil to serve sin. Instead, give yourselves completely to God, for you were dead, but now you have new life. So use your whole body as an instrument to do what is right for the glory of God. Sin is no longer your master, for you no longer live under the requirements of the law. Instead, you live under the freedom of God's grace.

ROMANS 6:12-14

Jesus said to his disciples, "If any of you wants to be my follower, you must turn from your selfish ways, take up your cross, and follow me. If you try to hang on to your life, you will lose it. But if you give up your life for my sake, you will save it."

MATTHEW 16:24-25

*O*ne of the oldest lies in the book is that you are a victim who has no power to resist some of the powerful influences around you. The world teaches you that your circumstances, heredity, or environment excuses you from responsibility. This no-fault policy actually leaves you vulnerable to being held captive by your sinful desires. But God is more powerful than anything that seeks to control you. When you try to control your own life, you usually end up losing control to other things. Wrong desires can easily sneak in and set up a routine of bad habits. Changing those habits isn't a means of taking back control but of giving up control—to God. You may feel your bad habits control you now, but your relationship with God gives you access to his transforming power. When you ask for his power through prayer and the support of his Spirit and fellow believers, God breaks the chains that hold you and sets you free from those controlling habits.

DIVINE PROMISE

MAKE EVERY EFFORT TO RESPOND TO GOD'S PROMISES. SUPPLEMENT YOUR FAITH WITH A GENEROUS PROVISION OF MORAL EXCELLENCE, AND MORAL EXCELLENCE WITH KNOWLEDGE, AND KNOWLEDGE WITH SELF-CONTROL, AND SELF-CONTROL WITH PATIENT ENDURANCE, AND PATIENT ENDURANCE WITH GODLINESS, AND GODLINESS WITH BROTHERLY AFFECTION, AND BROTHERLY AFFECTION WITH LOVE FOR EVERYONE. THE MORE YOU GROW LIKE THIS, THE MORE PRODUCTIVE AND USEFUL YOU WILL BE IN YOUR KNOWLEDGE OF OUR LORD JESUS CHRIST.   *2 Peter 1:5-8*

Hand of God

MY QUESTIONS *for* GOD

What is the "hand of God"? How can I see God's hand in my life?

A MOMENT *with* GOD

Come and see what our God has done, what awesome miracles he performs for people!   PSALM 66:5

It is the LORD who provides the sun to light the day and the moon and stars to light the night, and who stirs the sea into roaring waves. His name is the LORD of Heaven's Armies.   JEREMIAH 31:35

*P*eople often think of the hand of God when they see miraculous or unexplainable occurrences. And although it is true that God's hand is evident in those cases, we can also see his hand at work in the common, everyday blessings we enjoy. His fingerprints are all over nature: from the faithful rising of the sun and changing seasons to bountiful harvests and provisions for nourishment. The more you open your spiritual eyes and look around you, the more you will see God's hand at work and experience a sense of his divine presence.

DIVINE PROMISE

O LORD MY GOD, YOU HAVE PERFORMED MANY
WONDERS FOR US. YOUR PLANS FOR US ARE
TOO NUMEROUS TO LIST. YOU HAVE NO EQUAL.
IF I TRIED TO RECITE ALL YOUR WONDERFUL
DEEDS, I WOULD NEVER COME TO THE END
OF THEM.   *Psalm 40:5*

Heart

MY QUESTION *for* GOD

How do I protect my heart?

A MOMENT *with* GOD

Guard your heart above all else, for it determines the
course of your life.   PROVERBS 4:23

Dear children, keep away from anything that might
take God's place in your hearts.   1 JOHN 5:21

Christ will make his home in your hearts as you trust
in him. Your roots will grow down into God's love
and keep you strong.   EPHESIANS 3:17

My child, listen and be wise: Keep your heart on the
right course.   PROVERBS 23:19

The human heart is the vital organ that pumps blood
and oxygenates your body. When it doesn't function
properly, your body doesn't function properly. Doc-
tors encourage exercise and a nutritious diet to keep

your heart fit and healthy. In the Bible, the heart is also considered the center of thought and feeling. It is so important that God cautions you to guard it above all else, because your heart filters everything that happens to you. When you neglect your heart, it becomes filthy and clogged with all kinds of foulness that settles inside—bitterness, rage, impure thoughts. A dirty heart can no longer tell the good from the harmful and allows hurt and heartache to enter. When you keep your heart pure and clean, it can block the toxins of sinful desires and thoughts that threaten your spiritual health.

DIVINE PROMISE

GOD BLESSES THOSE WHOSE HEARTS ARE PURE, FOR THEY WILL SEE GOD.   *Matthew 5:8*

Heaven

MY QUESTION *for* GOD

How does heaven affect my life now?

A MOMENT *with* GOD

Our present troubles are small and won't last very long. Yet they produce for us a glory that vastly outweighs them and will last forever!

2 CORINTHIANS 4:17

God has made everything beautiful for its own time.
He has planted eternity in the human heart.

ECCLESIASTES 3:11

This world is not our permanent home; we are
looking forward to a home yet to come.   HEBREWS 13:14

*A*s a heaven-bound follower of God, try to put heaven
and earth in perspective. Here, you will probably live
for less than a hundred years. In heaven, one hundred
million years will just be the beginning. Yet amazingly,
God determined that how you live during your short
time on earth should prepare you for heaven. Knowing this infuses your life with purpose, gives you perspective on your troubles, and helps you anticipate the
unique role God has planned for you in eternity.

DIVINE PROMISE

OUR PRESENT TROUBLES ARE SMALL AND
WON'T LAST VERY LONG. YET THEY PRODUCE
FOR US A GLORY THAT VASTLY OUTWEIGHS
THEM AND WILL LAST FOREVER!   *2 Corinthians 4:17*

Help

MY QUESTION *for* GOD

*I can't do everything by myself. Where can I find the help
I need?*

A MOMENT *with* GOD

This same God who takes care of me will supply all
your needs from his glorious riches, which have been
given to us in Christ Jesus.   PHILIPPIANS 4:19

The LORD is my strength and shield. I trust him with
all my heart. He helps me, and my heart is filled with
joy. I burst out in songs of thanksgiving.   PSALM 28:7

The LORD God said, "It is not good for the man to be
alone. I will make a helper who is just right for him."
                                        GENESIS 2:18

Learn to do good. Seek justice. Help the oppressed.
Defend the cause of orphans. Fight for the rights of
widows.   ISAIAH 1:17

*E*veryone has limitations: areas of weakness, feelings
of inadequacy, lack of skill or knowledge. Sometimes
you just don't know what to do or how to do it. Sometimes a crisis strikes, and you just can't handle it by
yourself. You need help. Although the world may admire the strong, independent spirit, no one can really
survive alone. That's why God created you to be in relationship with him and with other people. Part of relationship is giving and receiving help. You need help to
get work done. You need help to restore a relationship.
You need help to develop your skills. You need help
thinking through a problem. You need help to say, "I'm
sorry." God wants to help you too. He is your ultimate
helper, for he is the wisest, strongest, and most loving.
Not only does your help come from God, but God also

promises to help those who help others. Cultivate the habits of seeking the help of both God and others and of offering help to those in need.

DIVINE PROMISE

COMMIT EVERYTHING YOU DO TO THE LORD. TRUST HIM, AND HE WILL HELP YOU.   *Psalm 37:5*

Hiding

MY QUESTION *for* GOD

Is God hiding himself and his plans from me?

A MOMENT *with* GOD

Ever since the world was created, people have seen the earth and sky. Through everything God made, they can clearly see his invisible qualities—his eternal power and divine nature. So they have no excuse for not knowing God.   ROMANS 1:20

You will search again for the LORD your God. And if you search for him with all your heart and soul, you will find him.   DEUTERONOMY 4:29

Solomon, my son, learn to know the God of your ancestors intimately. Worship and serve him with your whole heart and a willing mind. For the LORD sees every heart and knows every plan and thought.

If you seek him, you will find him. But if you forsake
him, he will reject you forever.   1 CHRONICLES 28:9

My heart has heard you say, "Come and talk with
me." And my heart responds, "LORD, I am coming."

PSALM 27:8

𝒢od wants you to know him and reveals himself in
many ways when you are looking for him. He reveals
himself through his creation, through his Word, and
even directly into your heart. When you try to hide
from God, it is easy to blame the distance between you
and God on him. But God is always trying to reveal
himself to you. Do you really want to find him? To find
him means you may face a radical life change. Are you
genuinely searching for God? Are you ready for what
you will discover?

DIVINE PROMISE

ALL THAT IS SECRET WILL EVENTUALLY BE
BROUGHT INTO THE OPEN, AND EVERYTHING
THAT IS CONCEALED WILL BE BROUGHT TO
LIGHT AND MADE KNOWN TO ALL. *Luke 8:17*

Holiness

MY QUESTION *for* GOD

What does it mean to be holy?

A Moment *with* God

Christ made us right with God; he made us pure and holy, and he freed us from sin.   1 CORINTHIANS 1:30

Even before he made the world, God loved us and chose us in Christ to be holy and without fault in his eyes.   EPHESIANS 1:4

You were cleansed; you were made holy; you were made right with God by calling on the name of the Lord Jesus Christ and by the Spirit of our God.

1 CORINTHIANS 6:11

*H*oliness is much more than the absence of sin; it is the practice of righteousness, purity, and godliness. Holiness means you are absolutely dedicated and devoted to God, distinct and separate from the world's way of living, and committed to right living and purity. God makes you holy by forgiving your sins. When you belong to him, he looks at you as if you had never sinned. But while he sees you as holy, you have not perfected holiness. You must still strive each day to be more holy—more like God—as you look forward to complete holiness in heaven.

Divine Promise

[GOD] HAS RECONCILED YOU TO HIMSELF THROUGH THE DEATH OF CHRIST IN HIS PHYSICAL BODY. AS A RESULT, HE HAS BROUGHT YOU INTO HIS OWN PRESENCE, AND YOU ARE

HOLY AND BLAMELESS AS YOU STAND BEFORE
HIM WITHOUT A SINGLE FAULT.   *Colossians 1:22*

Holy Spirit

MY QUESTION *for* GOD

How does the Holy Spirit—the presence of God—help me?

A MOMENT *with* GOD

We have received God's Spirit (not the world's
spirit), so we can know the wonderful things God has
freely given us.   1 CORINTHIANS 2:12

Let the Holy Spirit guide your lives. Then you won't
be doing what your sinful nature craves. The sinful
nature wants to do evil, which is just the opposite of
what the Spirit wants. And the Spirit gives us desires
that are the opposite of what the sinful nature desires.

GALATIANS 5:16-17

The Holy Spirit helps us in our weakness. For
example, we don't know what God wants us to pray
for. But the Holy Spirit prays for us with groanings
that cannot be expressed in words. And the Father
who knows all hearts knows what the Spirit is saying,
for the Spirit pleads for us believers in harmony with
God's own will.   ROMANS 8:26-27

The Holy Spirit helps you understand the deep truths
of God so that you can discover and know the mysteries

and wonders of his character. The Spirit also helps you know the truth about sin and makes you aware of it in your own heart and life. It is God in you that shows you right from wrong, good from bad. Finally, the Holy Spirit helps you pray. You can take great comfort and confidence in the fact that God hears and understands your prayers and responds to them. So often your soul longs to be recognized and understood, and yet you can't find the words. But the Holy Spirit understands the deepest longings of your heart and expresses them to God on your behalf.

DIVINE PROMISE

THE SPIRIT IS GOD'S GUARANTEE THAT HE WILL GIVE US THE INHERITANCE HE PROMISED AND THAT HE HAS PURCHASED US TO BE HIS OWN PEOPLE. HE DID THIS SO WE WOULD PRAISE AND GLORIFY HIM. *Ephesians 1:14*

Honesty

MY QUESTION *for* GOD

How does honesty help prepare me for God's purposes?

A MOMENT *with* GOD

All who cheat with dishonest weights and measures are detestable to the LORD your God.

DEUTERONOMY 25:16

The LORD detests double standards; he is not pleased by dishonest scales.   PROVERBS 20:23

The LORD demands accurate scales and balances; he sets the standards for fairness.   PROVERBS 16:11

If you are faithful in little things, you will be faithful in large ones. But if you are dishonest in little things, you won't be honest with greater responsibilities.

LUKE 16:10

*H*onesty matters greatly to God because it reveals your character. If you have developed the habit of cheating, it will be very difficult to stop when bigger challenges with bigger stakes come your way. It doesn't matter whether or not anyone else is watching—God is! Even if no one else knows, God knows, and he sees the true character that is revealed in those moments when you think no one is looking. If you can't be trusted to be honest in a small matter, you can't be trusted to be honest in a big matter. Honesty prepares you for responsibility. When you have built your life with bricks of honesty, you have a strong foundation for acting with integrity when great challenges and responsibility come your way. When God's standards of fairness and justice govern your life, you'll be ready to carry out God's purposes for your life.

DIVINE PROMISE

WHO MAY CLIMB THE MOUNTAIN OF THE
LORD? WHO MAY STAND IN HIS HOLY PLACE?
ONLY THOSE WHOSE HANDS AND HEARTS
ARE PURE, WHO DO NOT WORSHIP IDOLS
AND NEVER TELL LIES. THEY WILL RECEIVE
THE LORD'S BLESSING AND HAVE A RIGHT
RELATIONSHIP WITH GOD THEIR SAVIOR.

Psalm 24:3-5

Hope

MY QUESTION *for* GOD

How can I cultivate stronger hope?

A MOMENT *with* GOD

Do not snatch your word of truth from me, for your
regulations are my only hope. . . . May all who fear
you find in me a cause for joy, for I have put my hope
in your word. . . . I am worn out waiting for your
rescue, but I have put my hope in your word. . . . You
are my refuge and my shield; your word is my source
of hope. . . . I rise early, before the sun is up; I cry
out for help and put my hope in your words.

PSALM 119:43, 74, 81, 114, 147

Such things were written in the Scriptures long
ago to teach us. And the Scriptures give us hope
and encouragement as we wait patiently for God's
promises to be fulfilled.   ROMANS 15:4

All glory to God, who is able, through his mighty power at work within us, to accomplish infinitely more than we might ask or think.   EPHESIANS 3:20

*H*ope is cultivated as you read God's Word. Its stories and promises remind you of God's miraculous love and plan for his people. As you see how God's hand has worked in miraculous ways throughout history, you will find yourself gaining hope and confidence that he will work in your future as well. The Bible not only reminds you of God's past faithfulness but it also points to his future faithfulness in heaven. You will find encouragement and perspective as you learn to trust in God's promise of eternal life. Each day you can read God's Word and have your hope renewed and reinforced. As you review his promises for your future, you will find yourself joyfully anticipating each new day from now throughout eternity. Even in dark times, God's Word is able to lift you up.

DIVINE PROMISE

O LORD, YOU ALONE ARE MY HOPE.   *Psalm 71:5*

Humility

MY QUESTION *for* GOD

What does it mean to be humble?

A MOMENT *with* GOD

Those who are left will be the lowly and humble, for it is they who trust in the name of the LORD.

ZEPHANIAH 3:12

I recognize my rebellion; it haunts me day and night. Against you, and you alone, have I sinned; I have done what is evil in your sight. You will be proved right in what you say, and your judgment against me is just.

PSALM 51:3-4

Humility is the honest recognition of your own worth—your worth as God sees you. It is the delicate balance between honestly recognizing your sin and yet knowing how much God loves and values you. While pride elevates you above others and often above God himself, degrading your sense of self-worth is unacceptable for it denies the value God placed on you when he created you in his image and extended the offer of eternal life to you. God's gift isn't for "worms" but for people he loves very much. To see yourself as God sees you—that is your goal.

DIVINE PROMISE

THE HUMBLE WILL SEE THEIR GOD AT WORK AND BE GLAD. LET ALL WHO SEEK GOD'S HELP BE ENCOURAGED. *Psalm 69:32*

Humility

MY QUESTION *for* GOD

Why does God value a humble spirit?

A MOMENT *with* GOD

[God] gives us even more grace to stand against such
evil desires. As the Scriptures say, "God opposes the
proud but favors the humble." So humble yourselves
before God. Resist the devil, and he will flee from
you. Come close to God, and God will come close
to you. Wash your hands, you sinners; purify your
hearts, for your loyalty is divided between God and
the world. Let there be tears for what you have done.
Let there be sorrow and deep grief. Let there be
sadness instead of laughter, and gloom instead of joy.
Humble yourselves before the Lord, and he will lift
you up in honor.

JAMES 4:6-10

*H*umility is essential to recognizing the sin in your
life. Where pride gives the devil the key to your heart,
humility gives God your whole heart. In place of pride
is the humility that comes from godly sorrow over sin.
Openly admit that you need God, and seek his forgiveness, and you will do what no proud person could do.
When you give your whole heart to God, you open
yourself up to be used by God at all times and places!

DIVINE PROMISE

HUMBLE YOURSELVES UNDER THE MIGHTY POWER OF GOD, AND AT THE RIGHT TIME HE WILL LIFT YOU UP IN HONOR.   *1 Peter 5:6*

Hurt

MY QUESTION *for* GOD

How does God help me when I've been deeply hurt?

A MOMENT *with* GOD

I weep with sorrow; encourage me by your word. . . . Your promise revives me; it comforts me in all my troubles. . . . I meditate on your age-old regulations; O LORD, they comfort me. . . . If your instructions hadn't sustained me with joy, I would have died in my misery.   PSALM 119:28, 50-52, 92

We believers also groan, even though we have the Holy Spirit within us as a foretaste of future glory, for we long for our bodies to be released from sin and suffering. We, too, wait with eager hope for the day when God will give us our full rights as his adopted children, including the new bodies he has promised us.   ROMANS 8:23

He heals the brokenhearted and bandages their wounds.   PSALM 147:3

God does not promise you a life free from pain and suffering just because you believe in him. If those who believed in God never experienced hurts, other people would see God only as a magician who takes away pain. The difference is that you have a relationship with God, who helps you, comforts you, and sometimes even miraculously heals your hurts. But most important, you have a God who will take away all of your hurts when you arrive in heaven. Whatever pain you are experiencing is temporary. One day it will end, perhaps here on earth, but certainly in eternity.

DIVINE PROMISE

THOUGH [THE LORD] BRINGS GRIEF, HE ALSO SHOWS COMPASSION BECAUSE OF THE GREATNESS OF HIS UNFAILING LOVE. FOR HE DOES NOT ENJOY HURTING PEOPLE OR CAUSING THEM SORROW. *Lamentations 3:32-33*

Imagination

MY QUESTIONS *for* GOD

Why do we have the ability to be imaginative? Can our imagination ever be destructive?

A MOMENT *with* GOD

In the beginning God created. GENESIS 1:1

God created human beings in his own image.

GENESIS 1:27

Moses told the people of Israel, "The LORD has specifically chosen Bezalel. . . . The LORD has filled Bezalel with the Spirit of God, giving him great wisdom, ability, and expertise in all kinds of crafts."

EXODUS 35:30-31

God gave these four young men an unusual aptitude for understanding every aspect of literature and wisdom. And God gave Daniel the special ability to interpret the meanings of visions and dreams.

DANIEL 1:17

*O*ur God is a creative God, and he has made us in his image. If God was able to imagine the heavens and earth and animals and humans and a relationship with us, and we are patterned after him, then he has certainly instilled some imaginative abilities within us. Since God is the ultimate creator, he is the source of our creative abilities. Whether you use your imagination to paint a beautiful picture, design a building, or revolutionize how others think about God, your imagination can become an expression of gratitude to God for creating you in his image.

"My thoughts are nothing like your thoughts," says the LORD. "And my ways are far beyond anything you could imagine."

ISAIAH 55:8

The LORD observed the extent of human wickedness on the earth, and he saw that everything they thought or imagined was consistently and totally evil. So the

LORD was sorry he had ever made them and put them
on the earth. It broke his heart.   GENESIS 6:5-6

[Sinful, wicked people] invent new ways of sinning.
                                                 ROMANS 1:30

Those who are dominated by the sinful nature think
about sinful things, but those who are controlled
by the Holy Spirit think about things that please the
Spirit. So letting your sinful nature control your
mind leads to death. But letting the Spirit control
your mind leads to life and peace.   ROMANS 8:5-6

They said, "Come, let's build a great city for ourselves
with a tower that reaches into the sky. This will make
us famous and keep us from being scattered all over
the world." But the LORD came down to look at the
city and the tower the people were building. "Look!"
he said. "The people are united, and they all speak
the same language. After this, nothing they set out to
do will be impossible for them!"   GENESIS 11:4-6

These verses demonstrate the power of human imagination. While the tower of Babel was conceived out
of pride, the people's abilities to design and construct
such a tower suggests there are few limits to what the
human mind can imagine and implement. The human
imagination is powerful, and the dark side is that it can
easily be hijacked by your sinful nature. Because your
imagination is connected to your thought life, whatever controls your thoughts controls your imagination.
When your sinful nature controls you, selfish desires

control your mind, and your imagination can easily become a tool of destruction, concocting all kinds of ways to think only of yourself while hurting others. But when your thoughts are controlled by your new nature, your imagination is inspired by God's creative character and becomes a tool of healthy innovation and vision.

DIVINE PROMISE

FIX YOUR THOUGHTS ON WHAT IS TRUE, AND HONORABLE, AND RIGHT, AND PURE, AND LOVELY, AND ADMIRABLE. THINK ABOUT THINGS THAT ARE EXCELLENT AND WORTHY OF PRAISE. KEEP PUTTING INTO PRACTICE ALL YOU LEARNED AND RECEIVED FROM ME— EVERYTHING YOU HEARD FROM ME AND SAW ME DOING. THEN THE GOD OF PEACE WILL BE WITH YOU.   *Philippians 4:8-9*

Impossible

MY QUESTION *for* GOD

What is the key to experiencing the impossible in life?

A MOMENT *with* GOD

This is what the LORD of Heaven's Armies says: All this may seem impossible to you now, a small remnant of God's people. But is it impossible for me?

ZECHARIAH 8:6

"What do you mean, 'If I can'?" Jesus asked. "Anything is possible if a person believes."   MARK 9:23

"You don't have enough faith," Jesus told them. "I tell you the truth, if you had faith even as small as a mustard seed, you could say to this mountain, 'Move from here to there,' and it would move. Nothing would be impossible."   MATTHEW 17:20

The Bible is filled with seemingly impossible stories: A flood covers the earth. A sea is divided so people can walk through on dry land. The sun keeps shining until a battle can be won. A man survives three days in the belly of a fish. A virgin gives birth to a baby boy. To the person who does not believe in God or his Word, these stories defy logic. But those who believe in the Creator of all things also believe that he can alter what he has created; he can break into natural law and cause something supernatural. In order for you to recognize and experience the impossible, you need faith. Faith opens up a new dimension and allows you to understand that what you see is not all there is. Suddenly, you can recognize the "impossible" things God does for his people because you believe that anything is possible for him. Learn to recognize and appreciate the "impossible" things God does for you and around you each day: unexpected forgiveness, healing for the body and heart, the intricate systems of the human body, amazement at the exact conditions needed to support life on earth, or the birth of a baby. The more you see the "impossible" acts of God with eyes of faith, the stronger your faith in God will become.

DIVINE PROMISE

JESUS LOOKED AT THEM INTENTLY AND SAID, "HUMANLY SPEAKING, IT IS IMPOSSIBLE. BUT WITH GOD EVERYTHING IS POSSIBLE."
Matthew 19:26

Influence

MY QUESTION *for* GOD

Can I know if my life is counting for Jesus?

A MOMENT *with* GOD

God has given both his promise and his oath. These two things are unchangeable because it is impossible for God to lie. Therefore, we who have fled to him for refuge can have great confidence as we hold to the hope that lies before us. This hope is a strong and trustworthy anchor for our souls. It leads us through the curtain into God's inner sanctuary. HEBREWS 6:18-19

You may not be able to see how your life influences others on this side of eternity. You may be planting seeds of faith in the lives of people around you, and those seeds will grow into faith you will never even know about. Instead of trying to have influence, live every day—moment by moment—in obedience to God. The years of life built on daily obedience develop the character and integrity that draw others to Jesus.

DIVINE PROMISE

YOU KNOW OF OUR CONCERN FOR YOU FROM THE WAY WE LIVED WHEN WE WERE WITH YOU.
1 Thessalonians 1:5

Initiative

MY QUESTION *for* GOD

How does God initiate a relationship with me?

A MOMENT *with* GOD

If any of you wants to be my follower, you must turn from your selfish ways, take up your cross, and follow me. If you try to hang on to your life, you will lose it. But if you give up your life for my sake and for the sake of the Good News, you will save it.   MARK 8:34-35

Sometimes God initiates a change of heart in you so that you desire to have a relationship with him. Selfish ambition can blind you toward your sinful ways. God needs to point out these ways within you and convince you of your sinfulness in order to have an intimate relationship with you. But when God convicts you of wrongful ways, he also guides you back to the right path. He will never initiate a change of heart and then abandon you. God desires that you be a part of his work, and he will be with you, molding you into the kind of person he can use.

God loved the world so much that he gave his one and only Son, so that everyone who believes in him will not perish but have eternal life.   JOHN 3:16

God showed his great love for us by sending Christ to die for us while we were still sinners.   ROMANS 5:8

Since our friendship with God was restored by the death of his Son while we were still his enemies, we will certainly be saved through the life of his Son.

ROMANS 5:10

I have loved you, my people, with an everlasting love. With unfailing love I have drawn you to myself.

JEREMIAH 31:3

God initiated a relationship with you by giving up the life of his Son. By this act, he made it possible for you to be called his friend. Before Jesus died and rose again, your sins made it impossible for you to have a relationship with God. But because of his love, he made the first move. By the sacrifice he made for you, he extends his hand always. He offered you forgiveness before you were even born. And he gives you the gift of eternity even though you don't deserve it. He took the initiative to do these things for you because you are precious to him and he longs for a relationship with you.

DIVINE PROMISE

I WILL ANSWER THEM BEFORE THEY EVEN CALL
TO ME. WHILE THEY ARE STILL TALKING ABOUT
THEIR NEEDS, I WILL GO AHEAD AND ANSWER
THEIR PRAYERS!   *Isaiah 65:24*

Injustice

MY QUESTIONS *for* GOD

*Why does a loving, sovereign God allow injustice? If he
doesn't stop it, what am I supposed to do?*

A MOMENT *with* GOD

How long, O LORD, must I call for help? But you
do not listen! "Violence is everywhere!" I cry, but
you do not come to save. . . . But you are pure and
cannot stand the sight of evil. Will you wink at their
treachery? Should you be silent while the wicked
swallow up people more righteous than they?

HABAKKUK 1:2, 13

They twist justice in the courts—doesn't the Lord
see all these things?   LAMENTATIONS 3:36

I know the vast number of your sins and the depth of
your rebellions. You oppress good people by taking
bribes and deprive the poor of justice in the courts.

AMOS 5:12

Acquitting the guilty and condemning the
innocent—both are detestable to the LORD.

PROVERBS 17:15

Fear the LORD and judge with integrity, for the
LORD our God does not tolerate perverted justice,
partiality, or the taking of bribes.   2 CHRONICLES 19:7

𝒥njustice is the result of human beings' choices: God
created Adam and Eve with free will; that is, the freedom to choose good or evil, right or wrong. If God
hadn't done it that way, we would be only puppets of
a divine dictator, not people who love him. God knew
that people needed the freedom to choose, but that also
means that many will choose wrongly and cause injustice to the innocent. But to think that God condones
injustice simply because it exists is contrary to his righteous nature and opposed to what the Bible teaches
about all sin. God sees every injustice and judges it to
be sin. Leaders have a special responsibility not to look
the other way when injustice occurs among those they
lead. They must do their part to fight injustice. When
they do, they create divine moments, not only in the
lives of those they rescue, but also in the hearts of those
who are watching.

DIVINE PROMISE

THOSE WHO PLANT INJUSTICE WILL HARVEST
DISASTER, AND THEIR REIGN OF TERROR WILL
COME TO AN END.   *Proverbs 22:8*

Inspiration

My Question *for* God

How does God inspire people?

A Moment *with* God

Those who live at the ends of the earth stand in awe of your wonders. From where the sun rises to where it sets, you inspire shouts of joy. PSALM 65:8

All Scripture is inspired by God and is useful to teach us what is true and to make us realize what is wrong in our lives. It corrects us when we are wrong and teaches us to do what is right. 2 TIMOTHY 3:16

The Spirit of God has made me, and the breath of the Almighty gives me life. JOB 33:4

God inspires people in a variety of ways, but the most visible is through the beauty and variety of nature. He also inspires people through his Word, the Bible, with instruction, guidance, and correction. When you put your trust in Jesus, God gives the additional inspiration of the Holy Spirit, who inspires you with hope, comfort, wisdom, and love.

DIVINE PROMISE

WE HAVE RECEIVED GOD'S SPIRIT (NOT THE WORLD'S SPIRIT), SO WE CAN KNOW THE WONDERFUL THINGS GOD HAS FREELY GIVEN US. *1 Corinthians 2:12*

Integrity

MY QUESTION *for* GOD

What does it mean to live with integrity?

A MOMENT *with* GOD

If you are faithful in little things, you will be faithful
in large ones. But if you are dishonest in little things,
you won't be honest with greater responsibilities.

LUKE 16:10

[Pilate] announced his verdict. "You brought this
man to me, accusing him of leading a revolt. I have
examined him thoroughly on this point in your
presence and find him innocent. Herod came to the
same conclusion and sent him back to us. Nothing
this man has done calls for the death penalty."

LUKE 23:14-15

Integrity is the consistency of actions, character, and
beliefs. Integrity means knowing what you believe and
living as if you believe it. You build a reputation of integrity over time as you consistently demonstrate your
honest dependability through your words and your actions. No one models this better than Jesus. Although
you can never be perfect as he was, you can always
grow in integrity. This involves being faithful in every
area of your life, no matter how small. In fact, you'll
probably find that it is in the small things that your integrity will be tested the most. When your faithfulness
is tested, remember that each one of your actions has

consequences. What you do every day is forging your lasting reputation. Your actions moment by moment are developing the personal qualities by which you will be remembered. Then, at some point, you—or someone you love—will be in a desperate situation, and suddenly you will realize that your integrity is the only thing that will save the day. Because of your integrity people will trust you and look to you, you will do the right thing, and you will thank God that your integrity created a divine moment in which others can see Christ in you.

DIVINE PROMISE

TO THE FAITHFUL YOU SHOW YOURSELF FAITHFUL; TO THOSE WITH INTEGRITY YOU SHOW INTEGRITY. *2 Samuel 22:26*

Involvement

MY QUESTION *for* GOD

How can I know where God wants me to serve or be involved?

A MOMENT *with* GOD

Learn to do good. Seek justice. Help the oppressed. Defend the cause of orphans. Fight for the rights of widows. ISAIAH 1:17

Do not neglect the spiritual gift you received through the prophecy spoken over you when the elders of the church laid their hands on you. Give your complete attention to these matters. Throw yourself into your tasks so that everyone will see your progress.

1 TIMOTHY 4:14-15

All the believers devoted themselves to the apostles' teaching, and to fellowship, and to sharing in meals (including the Lord's Supper), and to prayer.   ACTS 2:42

You may not always have a specific calling to engage in, but there are many general tasks that God asks all believers to involve themselves in: taking care of God's creation and protecting the environment, caring for the needy in your church and community, defending and upholding justice, exercising your spiritual gifts for the service of the church, joining in worship and fellowship with other believers, and living as an example to those who do not know Christ. These are all ways that you can get involved in serving God right now! But sometimes God places a special need on your heart and urges you to get involved in a specific task. You may feel a tug on your heart, a passion for serving a group of people or a specific person, to volunteer at a soup kitchen or teach a Sunday school class. This may be God urging you to get involved in a specific task he has for you. In today's "mind your own business" culture, the courage to get involved will certainly get others' attention. But ironically, opportunities to get involved are also God's way of getting your attention. In getting involved, you may have a divine moment, or you may be the one to bring a divine moment to others as they experience God's perfect timing of help and hope.

DIVINE CHALLENGE

YOU ARE THE LIGHT OF THE WORLD—LIKE A CITY ON A HILLTOP THAT CANNOT BE HIDDEN. NO ONE LIGHTS A LAMP AND THEN PUTS IT UNDER A BASKET. INSTEAD, A LAMP IS PLACED ON A STAND, WHERE IT GIVES LIGHT TO EVERYONE IN THE HOUSE. IN THE SAME WAY, LET YOUR GOOD DEEDS SHINE OUT FOR ALL TO SEE, SO THAT EVERYONE WILL PRAISE YOUR HEAVENLY FATHER.   *Matthew 5:14-16*

Joy

MY QUESTION *for* GOD

Where does joy come from?

A MOMENT *with* GOD

We can rejoice in our wonderful new relationship with God because our Lord Jesus Christ has made us friends of God.   ROMANS 5:11

The LORD your God is living among you. He is a mighty savior. He will take delight in you with gladness. With his love, he will calm all your fears. He will rejoice over you with joyful songs.

ZEPHANIAH 3:17

Always be full of joy in the Lord. I say it again—
rejoice! Let everyone see that you are considerate in
all you do.   PHILIPPIANS 4:4-5

I have learned how to be content with whatever I
have. I know how to live on almost nothing or with
everything. I have learned the secret of living in every
situation, whether it is with a full stomach or empty,
with plenty or little.   PHILIPPIANS 4:11-12

*Y*ou are an emotional being because God created you
with feelings. It is not unusual or abnormal to experience
emotional and spiritual highs and lows, even in relatively
short periods of time. However, the joy and contentment
to which these verses refer run much deeper than the
emotions of the moment. Real joy is more than happiness. This kind of joy is like a strong current that runs
deep beneath the stormy surface of your feelings. In essence, joy is the celebration of walking with God. It is
a sense of security that can come only from being held
by an eternal God. It is peace, knowing God accepts
you for who you are and that he wants you in eternity
with him forever. You experience joy through the quiet
confidence that God is guiding you at all times and in
all things and through knowing that wherever he guides
you, you will have peace of mind. Your emotions can't
shake that kind of strong foundation, and they can't hang
on as long as that kind of experience.

DIVINE PROMISE

THOSE WHO LOOK TO HIM FOR HELP WILL BE
RADIANT WITH JOY; NO SHADOW OF SHAME
WILL DARKEN THEIR FACES. . . . TASTE AND SEE
THAT THE LORD IS GOOD. OH, THE JOYS OF
THOSE WHO TAKE REFUGE IN HIM! *Psalm 34:5, 8*

Judging Others

MY QUESTION *for* GOD

*What's the difference between judging others and offering
constructive criticism?*

A MOMENT *with* GOD

Do not judge others, and you will not be judged. For
you will be treated as you treat others. The standard
you use in judging is the standard by which you will
be judged. And why worry about a speck in your
friend's eye when you have a log in your own?

MATTHEW 7:1-3

Don't speak evil against each other, dear brothers and
sisters. If you criticize and judge each other, then you
are criticizing and judging God's law. But your job is to
obey the law, not to judge whether it applies to you.

JAMES 4:11

*O*ne coach berates a player publicly for making a mistake in a game. Another coach waits until the game is
over and tells the player privately how to avoid making

the same mistake again. Although no one likes criticism—even when it is constructive—we sometimes need it. But it is much easier to receive criticism when it is offered gently and in love rather than in a harsh or humiliating way. To judge someone is to criticize or find fault with someone without any effort to see that person succeed or improve. To offer constructive criticism is to invest in another for the purpose of building a relationship and helping that person become the person God created him or her to be. Being judgmental offers hurtful criticism that is not helpful; constructive criticism can be a divine moment of change.

DIVINE PROMISE

MAKE ALLOWANCE FOR EACH OTHER'S FAULTS, AND FORGIVE ANYONE WHO OFFENDS YOU. REMEMBER, THE LORD FORGAVE YOU, SO YOU MUST FORGIVE OTHERS. *Colossians 3:13*

Kindness

MY QUESTION *for* GOD

Can I experience God's kindness?

A MOMENT *with* GOD

[God] never left them without evidence of himself and his goodness. For instance, he sends you rain and good crops and gives you food and joyful hearts.

ACTS 14:17

Don't you see how wonderfully kind, tolerant, and patient God is with you? Does this mean nothing to you? Can't you see that his kindness is intended to turn you from your sin?   ROMANS 2:4

The LORD is merciful and compassionate, slow to get angry and filled with unfailing love. . . . The LORD is righteous in everything he does; he is filled with kindness.   PSALM 145:8, 17

Since it is through God's kindness, then it is not by their good works. For in that case, God's grace would not be what it really is—free and undeserved.

ROMANS 11:6

God's kindness is abundant and evident all around you, whether you notice it or not. First, God loves you unconditionally; that is, even when you don't deserve it. Second, he is patient and restrains his anger when you've sinned. He not only withholds the punishment you deserve but also forgives you and invites you into an eternal relationship with him. God also gives you time to turn from your sins and choose his way of life. When you do, he blesses you in both this life and the next. Finally, God's kindness is evident as he meets your needs. He provides for your physical needs as well as your spiritual needs. He sends the sun, rain, and harvests to care for you physically; he also sends spiritual refreshment to care for your soul. If you want to experience God's kindness, you simply need to become aware of all he has already provided.

DIVINE PROMISE

HOW KIND THE LORD IS! HOW GOOD HE IS! SO
MERCIFUL, THIS GOD OF OURS!   *Psalm 116:5*

Letting Go

MY QUESTION *for* GOD

How do I stop trying to control everything and learn to let go?

A MOMENT *with* GOD

Everything is wearisome beyond description. No
matter how much we see, we are never satisfied. No
matter how much we hear, we are not content.

ECCLESIASTES 1:8

I gave up in despair, questioning the value of all my
hard work in this world.   ECCLESIASTES 2:20

I know what enthusiasm they have for God, but it is
misdirected zeal. For they don't understand God's
way of making people right with himself. Refusing
to accept God's way, they cling to their own way of
getting right with God by trying to keep the law.
For Christ has already accomplished the purpose for
which the law was given. As a result, all who believe
in him are made right with God.   ROMANS 10:2-4

Learning to let go is one of the most important ways
to experience God's best for you. Learning to let go

doesn't mean embracing a void in your life but rather aligning your mind with God's plans for you and aligning your heart with his purpose for your life. It is only when you give up your will to God that you can be filled with his will. Frustration comes when you want to be in control, because then you are resisting God's work in your life. It's natural to want to control the outcome of your efforts, but when you do, you stunt God's ability to work through you. Letting go means that after you have done your best, you step back and trust God to complete the work he has asked you to start. Most important, you must learn to let go in order to receive God's salvation. Out of a natural desire to control life comes the idea that you can earn your way to heaven. Salvation, heaven, and eternity come from simple belief—they are gifts. As you learn to let go of your tendency of controlling your life, you find the freedom to experience the fullness of all of God's blessings to you.

DIVINE PROMISE

COMMIT YOUR ACTIONS TO THE LORD, AND YOUR PLANS WILL SUCCEED. *Proverbs 16:3*

Limitations

MY QUESTION *for* GOD

How do my limitations point to a limitless God?

A MOMENT *with* GOD

Have you never heard? Have you never understood?
The LORD is the everlasting God, the Creator of
all the earth. He never grows weak or weary.

ISAIAH 40:28

Jesus looked at them intently and said, "Humanly
speaking, it is impossible. But with God everything is
possible."   MATTHEW 19:26

My health may fail, and my spirit may grow weak,
but God remains the strength of my heart; he is mine
forever.   PSALM 73:26

Each time he said, "My grace is all you need. My
power works best in weakness." So now I am glad
to boast about my weaknesses, so that the power
of Christ can work through me. That's why I take
pleasure in my weaknesses, and in the insults,
hardships, persecutions, and troubles that I suffer
for Christ. For when I am weak, then I am strong.

2 CORINTHIANS 12:9-10

*I*n God's unlimited wisdom he created you with limitations—not to discourage you but to help you realize
your need for him. It is in your weakness that God's
strength shines. When you accomplish something great
despite your limitations, it is obvious that God was
working through you and that he deserves the credit.
God tells you that what is humanly impossible is possible
with him. The next time life makes you aware of your

limitations, instead of being discouraged, see it as an opportunity for God's power to defy your limitations.

DIVINE PROMISE

ALL GLORY TO GOD, WHO IS ABLE, THROUGH HIS MIGHTY POWER AT WORK WITHIN US, TO ACCOMPLISH INFINITELY MORE THAN WE MIGHT ASK OR THINK. *Ephesians 3:20*

Listening

MY QUESTION *for* GOD

How can I better listen to God?

A MOMENT *with* GOD

Each morning I bring my requests to you and wait expectantly. PSALM 5:3

Be still, and know that I am God! PSALM 46:10

Pay attention to how you hear. To those who listen to my teaching, more understanding will be given. But for those who are not listening, even what they think they understand will be taken away from them. LUKE 8:18

After the earthquake, there was a fire, but the LORD was not in the fire. And after the fire there was the sound of a gentle whisper. 1 KINGS 19:12

$\mathcal{L}$istening to people involves more than just hearing the sounds of their voices. You must observe, paying close attention to their body language, tone, and words in order to understand what the other person is really trying to communicate. It is similar when listening to God. First, come to God regularly and wait expectantly. God opens up more of himself as you demonstrate a faithful commitment to listening when he communicates. Find times to be quiet and meditate so that you will hear the voice of God when he speaks. Just as it's hard to pay attention to a conversation in a crowded room, it is also hard to hear God when you don't remove yourself from your daily distractions. God is big, so you might expect him to speak with the voice of thunder and lightning or earthquake or fire. But more often God expresses his powerful love in quiet, gentle whispers. Listen for him to speak to you personally in the quietness of your heart. Pay attention to the many ways in which God can speak to you, and don't miss an opportunity for communication with him. The more you listen to God, the more you will hear.

DIVINE PROMISE

MY CHILD, LISTEN TO WHAT I SAY, AND TREASURE MY COMMANDS. TUNE YOUR EARS TO WISDOM, AND CONCENTRATE ON UNDERSTANDING. CRY OUT FOR INSIGHT, AND ASK FOR UNDERSTANDING. SEARCH FOR THEM AS YOU WOULD FOR SILVER; SEEK THEM LIKE HIDDEN TREASURES. THEN YOU WILL UNDERSTAND WHAT IT MEANS TO FEAR THE LORD, AND YOU WILL GAIN KNOWLEDGE OF GOD. *Proverbs 2:1-5*

Loneliness

MY QUESTION for GOD

Why does God allow me to get lonely?

A MOMENT with GOD

The LORD God said, "It is not good for the man to be alone. I will make a helper who is just right for him."

GENESIS 2:18

I am convinced that nothing can ever separate us from God's love. Neither death nor life, neither angels nor demons, neither our fears for today nor our worries about tomorrow—not even the powers of hell can separate us from God's love. No power in the sky above or in the earth below—indeed, nothing in all creation will ever be able to separate us from the love of God that is revealed in Christ Jesus our Lord.

ROMANS 8:38-39

God created people for satisfying and meaningful relationships with himself and with others. It was not his intention for anyone to be lonely. It was God who recognized Adam's need for companionship. But because you live in an imperfect world, you will sometimes experience separation, hurt, and isolation—the opposite of all that God meant to be fulfilling in relationships. With the seasons of life, relationships make their entrances and exits. Perhaps you've been betrayed, or maybe your actions caused others to cut you off. Maybe friends have moved away, or no one seems to listen or care anymore. God allows people's actions in this life to take their natural course. Your feelings of loneliness can be the pathway to experiencing God's great love for you. There is no reason to feel sorry for yourself when God tells you that even the powers of hell can't hold back his love for you. Although life's circumstances may be less than ideal, you can count on friendship in the one relationship that will never end. God promises that when you belong to him, you may feel lonely sometimes, but you will never be alone.

DIVINE PROMISE

HOW PRECIOUS ARE YOUR THOUGHTS ABOUT ME, O GOD. THEY CANNOT BE NUMBERED! I CAN'T EVEN COUNT THEM; THEY OUTNUMBER THE GRAINS OF SAND! AND WHEN I WAKE UP, YOU ARE STILL WITH ME!   *Psalm 139:17-18*

Loss

MY QUESTION *for* GOD

How do I deal with the loss of a loved one?

A MOMENT *with* GOD

Joseph threw himself on his father and wept over him and kissed him. Then Joseph told the physicians who served him to embalm his father's body; so Jacob was embalmed. The embalming process took the usual forty days. And the Egyptians mourned his death for seventy days. . . . When they arrived at the threshing floor of Atad, near the Jordan River, they held a very great and solemn memorial service, with a seven-day period of mourning for Joseph's father.

GENESIS 50:1-3, 10

When the people who were at the house consoling Mary saw her leave so hastily, they assumed she was going to Lazarus's grave to weep. So they followed her there. . . . When Jesus saw her weeping and saw the other people wailing with her, a deep anger welled up within him, and he was deeply troubled. "Where have you put him?" he asked them. They told him, "Lord, come and see." Then Jesus wept. The people who were standing nearby said, "See how much he loved him!"

JOHN 11:31-36

God blesses those who mourn, for they will be comforted.

MATTHEW 5:4

You have turned my mourning into joyful dancing. You have taken away my clothes of mourning and clothed me with joy, that I might sing praises to you and not be silent. O LORD my God, I will give you thanks forever!

PSALM 30:11-12

Human grief typically involves stages of shock, anger, and depression before someone can move into resolution and acceptance. When Jacob thought his son Joseph was dead (see Genesis 37:34-35), he became stuck in his grief. When we deny ourselves the time to go through the stages of grief, the same thing can happen to us, and our pain may never be resolved. This story affirms that the process of grief is legitimate and that we must respect it. When Jacob dies, Joseph goes through the initial shock and overwhelming grief, preparation of and participation in funeral and memorial services, and finally closure as his father is buried. Although we are centuries and cultures removed, grief today is just as real. We must respect the way God created us and welcome his guidance and presence in our process of grieving. We must also be patient with those who are grieving, show them compassion, and allow them time to move through the process. Although we know that certain losses are inevitable, loss always bring pain. Recognizing and expressing that pain is not wrong or sinful; rather it is a healthy expression of how God created us. Don't deny the losses in your life. Great grief is the expression of great love. Express your feelings honestly to the Lord. He is not surprised and will not reject you when you cry out in your pain. Jesus' tears at Lazarus's death forever validate your tears of grief.

DIVINE PROMISE

THE LORD IS CLOSE TO THE BROKENHEARTED;
HE RESCUES THOSE WHOSE SPIRITS
ARE CRUSHED. *Psalm 34:18*

Love

MY QUESTION *for* GOD

What does genuine love for others look like?

A MOMENT *with* GOD

Love is patient and kind. Love is not jealous or boastful or proud or rude. It does not demand its own way. It is not irritable, and it keeps no record of being wronged. It does not rejoice about injustice but rejoices whenever the truth wins out. Love never gives up, never loses faith, is always hopeful, and endures through every circumstance.

1 CORINTHIANS 13:4-7

Love covers a multitude of sins.

1 PETER 4:8

There is no greater love than to lay down one's life for one's friends.

JOHN 15:13

*L*ove is not just about romance; in fact, it is not based primarily on feelings at all. Love is more a reflection of commitment to someone. It is not dependent on warm feelings but on a consistent and sacrificial decision to extend yourself for the well-being of another. That commitment then produces feelings of love, not the other way around. Understanding this kind of commitment as you love others is a window into understanding God's eternal commitment of love for you. Love is an act of spiritual maturity based on the eternal significance of another person. When you learn to see others as God sees them, even those you dislike or who dislike you, you will be able to love them. Love isn't about receiving gifts or pleasurable experiences. Love isn't about what you get out of it. Genuine love bubbles over from a spirit of giving and sacrifice. Love is willing to sacrifice for the good of others, even to death. Would you be willing to give up your very life for the chance that another might come to know Jesus? This is the genuine love of God at work in you!

DIVINE PROMISE

I AM GIVING YOU A NEW COMMANDMENT: LOVE EACH OTHER. JUST AS I HAVE LOVED YOU, YOU SHOULD LOVE EACH OTHER. YOUR LOVE FOR ONE ANOTHER WILL PROVE TO THE WORLD THAT YOU ARE MY DISCIPLES. *John 13:34-35*

Marriage

MY QUESTION *for* GOD

What are the keys to a happy, strong marriage?

A MOMENT *with* GOD

Choose today whom you will serve. . . . But as for me and my family, we will serve the LORD.   JOSHUA 24:15

Can two people walk together without agreeing on the direction?   AMOS 3:3

A shared purpose to serve the Lord is key to a strong marriage. If you want to take a walk with someone, you must decide together on the direction. If you want to walk through life with your spouse, you must decide together which direction you want to go: toward God and eternity with him or away. A unified commitment to walking with God is the key to experiencing daily divine moments together.

Since they are no longer two but one, let no one split apart what God has joined together.   MATTHEW 19:6

Commitment to stay together no matter what is essential for a strong and lasting relationship. If you leave open the option for splitting up some day, chances are you will. If you don't see breaking up as an option, you will be committed to making your marriage work in all circumstances. This commitment joins you together in pursuing and accomplishing united lifelong goals.

We must not just please ourselves. We should help others do what is right and build them up in the Lord.

ROMANS 15:1-2

Self-sacrifice is essential to a strong marriage. This means thinking of your spouse's needs and interests first. Who wouldn't want to be in a relationship where a husband or wife is always putting the other's needs ahead of his or her own?

May God, who gives this patience and encouragement, help you live in complete harmony with each other, as is fitting for followers of Christ Jesus. Then all of you can join together with one voice, giving praise and glory to God.   ROMANS 15:5-6

*U*nderstand each other's differences and celebrate them. This fosters respect for each other and turns differences that would normally annoy or distract you into unique strengths that interest and help you.

Let your conversation be gracious and attractive so that you will have the right response for everyone.

COLOSSIANS 4:6

Our letters have been straightforward, and there is nothing written between the lines and nothing you can't understand. I hope someday you will fully understand us, even if you don't understand us now.

2 CORINTHIANS 1:13-14

*C*ommunication is also necessary for strong and happy marriage. Since mind reading is possible only for God, talk to your spouse, and keep the lines of communication open, even when the conversation is awkward or hard. Instead of expecting the other person to guess what you're thinking, be honest. This will build trust and openness in your relationship.

The husband should fulfill his wife's sexual needs, and the wife should fulfill her husband's needs.

1 CORINTHIANS 7:3

Kiss me and kiss me again, for your love is sweeter than wine. . . . Take me with you; come, let's run! . . . My lover is like a sachet of myrrh lying between my breasts.   SONG OF SONGS 1:2-4, 13

*H*ealthy romance and physical love are important for a strong and happy marriage because they allow you to express intimacy and vulnerability in a way different from any other relationship. They foster special closeness that demonstrates your complete openness to each other. This is what sets marriage apart as a committed relationship like no other and makes it a symbol of your relationship with God.

DIVINE PROMISE

THE SCRIPTURES SAY, "A MAN LEAVES HIS FATHER AND MOTHER AND IS JOINED TO HIS WIFE, AND THE TWO ARE UNITED INTO ONE."
Ephesians 5:31

Meaning

MY QUESTION *for* GOD

How can I find more meaning in my life?

A MOMENT *with* GOD

Tune your ears to wisdom, and concentrate on understanding. Cry out for insight, and ask for understanding. Search for them as you would for silver; seek them like hidden treasures. PROVERBS 2:2-4

Fear of the LORD is the foundation of true wisdom. All who obey his commandments will grow in wisdom. Praise him forever! PSALM 111:10

Your commandments give me understanding; no wonder I hate every false way of life.   PSALM 119:104

I cry out to God Most High, to God who will fulfill his purpose for me.   PSALM 57:2

*C*hances are you won't just stumble onto the one thing that truly brings meaning and purpose to your life. You will have to search for it. Where do you start? Try doing everything you can to find God. When you do, you will discover the purpose for which he created you. Only God, the creator of life, can teach you how to live your life in a meaningful way. So pursue God in prayer; ask him to reveal his truth to you and to fulfill his purpose in you. God will not fail to use you for his purpose if you give yourself to him completely. Only God's purpose for you will satisfy you because he created you specifically for that purpose. Pursuit of anything else will always leave you empty.

DIVINE PROMISE

THE THIEF'S PURPOSE IS TO STEAL AND KILL AND DESTROY. MY PURPOSE IS TO GIVE THEM A RICH AND SATISFYING LIFE. *John 10:10*

Meditation

MY QUESTION *for* GOD

How can meditating help me in my spiritual walk?

A MOMENT *with* GOD

I wait quietly before God, for my victory comes from
him. . . . Let all that I am wait quietly before God,
for my hope is in him.   PSALM 62:1, 5

You must commit yourselves wholeheartedly to these
commands that I am giving you today. . . . Tie them
to your hands and wear them on your forehead as
reminders. Write them on the doorposts of your
house and on your gates.   DEUTERONOMY 6:6-9

I remember the days of old. I ponder all your great
works and think about what you have done. . . . Let
me hear of your unfailing love each morning, for I
am trusting you. Show me where to walk, for I give
myself to you. . . . Teach me to do your will, for
you are my God. May your gracious Spirit lead me
forward on a firm footing.   PSALM 143:5, 8-10

*M*editation is setting aside time to intentionally think
about God, talk to him, listen to him, read his Word,
and study the writings of devout men and women. If
you say you believe in a great and loving God but spend
no time connecting with him, how can you expect to
know what he wants from you? Could the problem be
that you're afraid to discover what he wants from you?
Because God is good, you can be assured that he wants
only his best for you. Meditation connects you with
God, restoring your hope in his promises, your vision
for what he has called you to do, and your commitment to follow him daily. When you meditate on God's

Word, you remember who he is and what he has done, and you gain confidence that he has so much yet in store for you. You remember him as the One who helps you fight and win in life's battles. Meditation weaves God into the fabric of your life so that you will be able to see him at work in everything you do. When you make the time to really listen to God, you remove yourself from the distractions and noise of the world around you and move within range of his voice. You prepare yourself to be teachable and to have your desires molded into his. As a result, your thoughts and your actions fall more in line with his commands. Meditation goes beyond the study of God to communion with him that ultimately conforms you more to his image.

DIVINE PROMISE

THINK ABOUT WHAT I AM SAYING. THE LORD WILL HELP YOU UNDERSTAND ALL THESE THINGS.   *2 Timothy 2:7*

Mercy

MY QUESTIONS *for* GOD

What is mercy? Why do I need it?

A MOMENT *with* GOD

The LORD is compassionate and merciful, slow to get angry and filled with unfailing love. He will not constantly accuse us, nor remain angry forever. He

does not punish us for all our sins; he does not deal
harshly with us, as we deserve.   PSALM 103:8-10

All praise to God, the Father of our Lord Jesus
Christ. It is by his great mercy that we have been
born again, because God raised Jesus Christ from
the dead.   1 PETER 1:3

The faithful love of the LORD never ends! His mercies
never cease. Great is his faithfulness; his mercies
begin afresh each morning.   LAMENTATIONS 3:22-23

Mercy is being spared what you rightly deserve.
God pours out his compassion on people who should
receive his anger and judgment but instead receive
grace. God's mercy goes one step further. It is more
than exemption from the punishment you deserve for
your sins. It is also receiving an undeserved gift—salvation from eternal death, and life forever in heaven.
Although you don't deserve God's mercy, he still extends it to you. Your rebellion against God deserves
his punishment; instead, he offers you forgiveness and
eternal life. Even more, God's mercies never end. He
never stops giving you his undivided attention, faithful
presence, spiritual gifts, provision for your needs, and
hope for your future—all undeserved and yet lavishly
poured out in your life. It is by his mercies that your
very life is sustained. It is a divine moment when you
realize your very breath is a merciful gift from an all-
loving God.

DIVINE PROMISE

THE FAITHFUL LOVE OF THE LORD NEVER
ENDS! HIS MERCIES NEVER CEASE. GREAT IS HIS
FAITHFULNESS; HIS MERCIES BEGIN AFRESH
EACH MORNING.   *Lamentations 3:22-23*

Miracles

MY QUESTIONS *for* GOD

*Does God still perform miracles today? How can I see more
miracles in my life?*

A MOMENT *with* GOD

Moses and Aaron did just as the LORD had
commanded them. When Aaron raised his hand and
struck the ground with his staff, gnats infested the
entire land, covering the Egyptians and their animals.
All the dust in the land of Egypt turned into gnats.
Pharaoh's magicians tried to do the same thing with
their secret arts, but this time they failed. And the
gnats covered everyone, people and animals alike.
"This is the finger of God!" the magicians exclaimed
to Pharaoh. But Pharaoh's heart remained hard.
He wouldn't listen to them, just as the LORD had
predicted.   EXODUS 8:17-19

Come and see what our God has done, what awesome
miracles he performs for people!   PSALM 66:5

The miracles of God recorded in the Bible can seem to be ancient myths if you fail to recognize God's intervention in your life today. Just as Pharaoh was blind to the miracles God performed right before his eyes through Moses, you, too, can blind yourself to God's miracles and fail to notice the mighty work he is doing all around you. Maybe you think a miracle is always a dramatic event like raising the dead. But miracles are happening all around you. These supernatural occurrences may not be as dramatic as the parting of the Red Sea, but they are no less powerful. When you look for God, he shows himself in miraculous ways: a breathtaking sunset, the restoration of a broken relationship, the birth of a baby, the healing of an illness, the rebirth of the earth in spring, salvation by faith in Jesus alone, the work of love and forgiveness that changes someone, hearing the specific call of God in your life. These are just a few of the miracles happening all the time. You have a miracle-working God who is able—and willing—to do the impossible in order to help you do his work. This means that no situation is hopeless. God encourages you to pray big prayers and never lose hope. If you think you've never seen a miracle, look closer.

DIVINE PROMISE

NO PAGAN GOD IS LIKE YOU, O LORD. NONE CAN DO WHAT YOU DO! *Psalm 86:8*

Mistakes

MY QUESTION *for* GOD

How do I move on after I've made a big mistake?

A MOMENT *with* GOD

If we claim we have not sinned, we are calling God a liar and showing that his word has no place in our hearts.

1 JOHN 1:10

If we confess our sins to him, he is faithful and just to forgive us our sins and to cleanse us from all wickedness.

1 JOHN 1:9

I don't mean to say that I have already achieved these things or that I have already reached perfection. But I press on to possess that perfection for which Christ Jesus first possessed me. No, dear brothers and sisters, I have not achieved it, but I focus on this one thing: forgetting the past and looking forward to what lies ahead.

PHILIPPIANS 3:12-13

Refusing to admit your mistakes locks you in the past. Acknowledging your faults releases you to be forgiven and to make things right. It's true that you need to learn from your mistakes, but you're not required to live by them. When you admit your mistakes, you demonstrate that you are a work in progress, living by God's grace. Once you admit your mistake, you are open to God's forgiveness. You may feel your sins are too great or too numerous to be forgiven, but God's forgiveness is not dependent on whether you think you deserve it or not. It is not dependent on the size or multitude of your sins. God wants to give forgiveness as much as you need to receive it. You just need to ask. Then, when you're forgiven, focus forward! Don't linger on your past. The door of the future is too small for the baggage of your past to fit through. Let it go, and walk through it into a new beginning.

DIVINE PROMISE

WHEN I REFUSED TO CONFESS MY SIN, MY BODY WASTED AWAY, AND I GROANED ALL DAY LONG. . . . FINALLY, I CONFESSED ALL MY SINS TO YOU AND STOPPED TRYING TO HIDE MY GUILT. I SAID TO MYSELF, "I WILL CONFESS MY REBELLION TO THE LORD." AND YOU FORGAVE ME! ALL MY GUILT IS GONE. *Psalm 32:3-5*

Motivation

MY QUESTION *for* GOD

How do I stay motivated when I am discouraged?

A MOMENT *with* GOD

If I say I'll never mention the LORD or speak in his name, his word burns in my heart like a fire. It's like a fire in my bones! I am worn out trying to hold it in!

JEREMIAH 20:9

Since God in his mercy has given us this new way, we
never give up.   2 CORINTHIANS 4:1

Don't copy the behavior and customs of this world,
but let God transform you into a new person by
changing the way you think. Then you will learn to
know God's will for you, which is good and pleasing
and perfect.   ROMANS 12:2

My life is worth nothing to me unless I use it for
finishing the work assigned me by the Lord Jesus.

                                          ACTS 20:24

*W*hen you nurture your relationship with God, all
that he gives you—work, blessings, commands, call-
ings—becomes like a burning passion within. Even
when you try to resist it or escape it, you cannot. The
closer you are to God, the more he gives you a clear,
ever-growing vision for your future and your part in
his eternal plan. Often lack of motivation comes from
lack of purpose. But God's purposes infuse your life
with energy and confidence as you trust him. When
you're feeling discouraged, let your sense of God's
presence, God's call, and God's love sustain you, even
when outward circumstances threaten to crush you. By
focusing on these things, you secure God's purpose in
your mind and heart, pushing you to fulfill all he has
planned for you. It is anticipation for your future that
compels you to move forward today.

DIVINE PROMISE

SEEK THE KINGDOM OF GOD ABOVE ALL ELSE,
AND LIVE RIGHTEOUSLY, AND HE WILL GIVE
YOU EVERYTHING YOU NEED.   *Matthew 6:33*

Motives

MY QUESTION *for* GOD

*As long as I do the right thing, what difference do my
motives make?*

A MOMENT *with* GOD

The LORD accepted Abel and his gift, but he did not
accept Cain and his gift.   GENESIS 4:4-5

The sacrifice of an evil person is detestable, especially
when it is offered with wrong motives.   PROVERBS 21:27

Even when you ask, you don't get it because your
motives are all wrong—you want only what will give
you pleasure.   JAMES 4:3

Your motives are everything to God. The condition
of your heart is essential to the condition of your relationship with him. Coming to God out of obligation,
or just to keep him from getting angry at you, or to
placate him to get something you really want shows
that you want a relationship with God for the wrong
reasons. Coming to God with a humble desire to know
him and what he wants for you is more about loving

and pleasing him than yourself. It is quite likely that God rejected Cain's sacrifice because Cain's motives were self-centered. When your motives are selfish, even seemingly right behavior can appear inappropriate. Don't let right actions be wasted by wrong motives. You will soon find your actions to be futile. But right motives always produce meaningful action, even in the smallest things. More important, when you pursue spiritual life with self-serving motives, you rob yourself of the joy God intends.

DIVINE PROMISE

I, THE LORD, SEARCH ALL HEARTS AND EXAMINE SECRET MOTIVES. I GIVE ALL PEOPLE THEIR DUE REWARDS, ACCORDING TO WHAT THEIR ACTIONS DESERVE.   *Jeremiah 17:10*

Motives

MY QUESTION *for* GOD

What are some of the ways God challenges my motives?

A MOMENT *with* GOD

Looking at the man, Jesus felt genuine love for him. "There is still one thing you haven't done," he told him. "Go and sell all your possessions and give the money to the poor, and you will have treasure in heaven. Then come, follow me." At this the man's

face fell, and he went away very sad, for he had many
possessions.   MARK 10:21-22

Put me on trial, LORD, and cross-examine me. Test
my motives and my heart.   PSALM 26:2

Search me, O God, and know my heart; test me and
know my anxious thoughts.   PSALM 139:23

*G*od challenges you to take the "heart" test. He wants
you to examine your heart; that is, to test your motives
to discover what you value most. If God is usually an
afterthought for you, if you give just a little time or
money to your church and to God's work, you need to
ask whether or not you are passing his test. Another
part of the "heart" test is how you react to problems
that interrupt your life. Do they drive you to ask God
for help, or do you usually try to solve them without
even thinking about God? Perhaps the biggest part of
the test is to ask yourself how you would respond if
God asked you to give away everything you have to
follow him. These are some of the ways God challenges
us. How are you handling the test?

DIVINE PROMISE

I WILL GIVE YOU A NEW HEART, AND I WILL
PUT A NEW SPIRIT IN YOU. I WILL TAKE OUT
YOUR STONY, STUBBORN HEART AND GIVE YOU
A TENDER, RESPONSIVE HEART.   *Ezekiel 36:26*

Music

MY QUESTION *for* GOD

How does music affect the way I worship God?

A MOMENT *with* GOD

Moses and the people of Israel sang this song to the
LORD: "I will sing to the LORD, for he has triumphed
gloriously; he has hurled both horse and rider into the
sea. The LORD is my strength and my song; he has
given me victory. This is my God, and I will praise
him—my father's God, and I will exalt him!"

EXODUS 15:1-2

Praise the LORD! How good to sing praises to our
God! How delightful and how fitting!   PSALM 147:1

The beauty and harmony of music are a testimony of
the glory and majesty of God. It is true that the lyrics
you sing point to God; the very beauty of the notes and
sounds touches your heart in a way that simple words
or readings cannot. They give a glimpse into the awesome creative beauty of God himself. For centuries,
music has played an essential role in expressing worship
of God. After the Israelites were rescued by God from
the Egyptians, they composed a song to express their
joy and gratitude to him for their deliverance. While
music can be an expressive outlet of faith, it can also
be a practical tool for teaching and remembering the
truths of God. Music can help you worship God by
retelling the stories of his greatness. Singing hymns

and songs is also a testimony and expression of your gratitude and praise and brings you into God's presence in a unique way. When evil hears God's people singing it will likely stay away, for evil has no desire to come near the presence of almighty God.

DIVINE PROMISE

THOSE WHO HAVE BEEN RANSOMED BY THE LORD WILL RETURN. THEY WILL ENTER JERUSALEM SINGING, CROWNED WITH EVERLASTING JOY. SORROW AND MOURNING WILL DISAPPEAR, AND THEY WILL BE FILLED WITH JOY AND GLADNESS.   *Isaiah 51:11*

Mystery

MY QUESTIONS *for* GOD

Why doesn't God make everything more clear? Why does he keep so many mysteries?

A MOMENT *with* GOD

The LORD replied, "I will make all my goodness pass before you, and I will call out my name, Yahweh, before you. For I will show mercy to anyone I choose, and I will show compassion to anyone I choose. But you may not look directly at my face, for no one may see me and live."   EXODUS 33:19-20

The LORD our God has secrets known to no one. We are not accountable for them, but we and our

children are accountable forever for all that he has
revealed to us, so that we may obey all the terms of
these instructions.   DEUTERONOMY 29:29

There are mysteries about God that the human mind
can never comprehend. God may hide these mysterious
truths from you because you cannot understand them
in your human condition and he is waiting to reveal
some of them in heaven, where your renewed mind can
handle them. He may also hide himself for your protection as he did with Moses. The extent of his power
and glory are so great that it would kill you to see God
face-to-face while you are in your human body. In any
case, God's reason for withholding certain knowledge
from you is not to frustrate you but rather to protect
you. Even when you arrive in heaven, you will forever
be discovering more and more about God. But this
shouldn't discourage you. God's mysteries are also opportunities for faith. If you knew everything there was
to know about God or his plans for your life, there
would be no need for faith. God has given you all you
need to know in order to believe in him. In your pursuit of the mysteries of God, don't let yourself forget
all that God has already revealed about himself to you.
You are not responsible for what you don't know about
God, but you are responsible to use what you do know
to obey and worship him and to serve others.

Divine Promise

HIS PURPOSE WAS FOR THE NATIONS TO SEEK
AFTER GOD AND PERHAPS FEEL THEIR WAY
TOWARD HIM AND FIND HIM—THOUGH HE IS
NOT FAR FROM ANY ONE OF US. FOR IN HIM
WE LIVE AND MOVE AND EXIST. *Acts 17:27-28*

Needs

My Question *for* God

*How will I grow in faith as I learn to distinguish my needs
from my wants?*

A Moment *with* God

Each time he said, "My grace is all you need. My
power works best in weakness." So now I am glad
to boast about my weaknesses, so that the power of
Christ can work through me.   2 Corinthians 12:9

If we have enough food and clothing, let us be
content.   1 Timothy 6:8

I have learned how to be content with whatever
I have.   Philippians 4:11

Don't love money; be satisfied with what you have.
For God has said, "I will never fail you. I will never
abandon you."   Hebrews 13:5

First, help me never to tell a lie. Second, give me
neither poverty nor riches! Give me just enough to
satisfy my needs.   Proverbs 30:8

Don't be like them, because your Father knows
exactly what you need even before you ask him. . . .
Your heavenly Father already knows all your needs.

MATTHEW 6:8, 32

I can do everything through Christ, who gives me
strength.   PHILIPPIANS 4:13

All humans have basic needs that must be met in order to survive: food, water, shelter, and love. Needs
are different from "wants" in that when your needs
are met, you can be content and satisfied. Wants, even
when fulfilled, often leave you unsatisfied, discontent,
and desiring more. Wants are not always negative, but
left unchecked, they can become fuel for the fires of
jealousy, envy, deceit, and materialism when you become obsessed with getting them. Your needs allow
God to show his power and provision and teach you
that he is sufficient. Learning to recognize the difference between needs and wants allows you to find contentment in living by God's way. The more you focus
on what the Lord values, the more you will be able to
distinguish your wants from your needs. If you constantly feel discontented, you may be focusing more on
what you want than on what God knows you need.

DIVINE PROMISE

GOD BLESSES THOSE WHO ARE POOR AND
REALIZE THEIR NEED FOR HIM, FOR THE
KINGDOM OF HEAVEN IS THEIRS. *Matthew 5:3*

Neglect

MY QUESTION for GOD

How do I neglect God?

A MOMENT with GOD

I immediately confronted the leaders and demanded, "Why has the Temple of God been neglected?" Then I called all the Levites back again and restored them to their proper duties.   NEHEMIAH 13:11

Let us not neglect our meeting together, as some people do, but encourage one another, especially now that the day of his return is drawing near.

HEBREWS 10:25

You neglect God and miss out on his divine moments when you neglect meeting together as a group of believers to worship him and serve each other.

Anyone who hears my teaching and doesn't obey it is foolish, like a person who builds a house on sand.

MATTHEW 7:26

We must listen very carefully to the truth we have heard, or we may drift away from it.   HEBREWS 2:1

This regular reading . . . will also prevent him from turning away from these commands in the smallest way.   DEUTERONOMY 17:20

*Y*ou neglect God when you ignore his Word, the Bible.

What makes us think we can escape if we ignore this great salvation that was first announced by the Lord Jesus himself and then delivered to us by those who heard him speak?   HEBREWS 2:3

Don't be misled—you cannot mock the justice of God. You will always harvest what you plant.

GALATIANS 6:7

*Y*ou neglect God when you ignore his offer of salvation.

Remember, it is sin to know what you ought to do and then not do it.   JAMES 4:17

*Y*ou neglect God when you ignore what you know is right, because you are neglecting God's commands for you.

DIVINE PROMISE

LOOK AFTER EACH OTHER SO THAT NONE OF YOU FAILS TO RECEIVE THE GRACE OF GOD. WATCH OUT THAT NO POISONOUS ROOT OF BITTERNESS GROWS UP TO TROUBLE YOU, CORRUPTING MANY. *Hebrews 12:15*

Neighbors

MY QUESTION *for* GOD

Who are my neighbors?

A MOMENT *with* GOD

The man wanted to justify his actions, so he asked Jesus, "And who is my neighbor?" Jesus replied with a story: "A Jewish man was traveling on a trip from Jerusalem to Jericho, and he was attacked by bandits. They stripped him of his clothes, beat him up, and left him half dead beside the road. By chance a priest came along . . . and passed him by. A Temple assistant walked over and looked at him lying there, but he also passed by on the other side. Then a despised Samaritan came along, and when he saw the man, he felt compassion for him. Going over to him, the Samaritan soothed his wounds with olive oil and wine and bandaged them. . . . Now which of these three would you say was a neighbor to the man who was attacked by bandits?" Jesus asked. The man replied, "The one who showed him mercy." Then Jesus said, "Yes, now go and do the same."

LUKE 10:29-37

*M*ost of us think of our neighbors as the people who live next door or across the street. Jesus' teachings expand your neighborhood to involve anyone around you who needs his love. This means that the person next to you on the plane, or your coworkers, or the homeless in your town are also your neighbors. It is also important to expand your neighborhood to people around the world who need the love of Christ. When you begin to view people you see or meet or even hear about as your neighbors, you see these encounters as divine opportunities, moments to share the love of Jesus by offering a helping hand. What neighbors have crossed your path today?

DIVINE PROMISE

INDEED, IT IS GOOD WHEN YOU OBEY THE
ROYAL LAW AS FOUND IN THE SCRIPTURES:
"LOVE YOUR NEIGHBOR AS YOURSELF."
James 2:8

Obedience

MY QUESTIONS *for* GOD

Do I have to obey everything God says? Isn't just believing in him enough?

A MOMENT *with* GOD

Now, Israel, what does the LORD your God require of you? He requires only that you fear the LORD your God, and live in a way that pleases him, and love him and serve him with all your heart and soul. And you must always obey the LORD's commands and decrees that I am giving you today for your own good.

DEUTERONOMY 10:12-13

Do what is right and good in the LORD's sight, so all will go well with you.   DEUTERONOMY 6:18

If you love me, obey my commandments.   JOHN 14:15

We live in a web of relationships dependent on obedience to authority. Like a loving parent or a responsible government, God sets standards for your good to protect you from evil and harm. God desires obedience motivated by love and trust, not by fear. Some people defy authority, but ironically, obedience actually frees you to enjoy life as God intended because it keeps you from becoming entangled in or enslaved to harmful situations that cause you heartache. The right thing to do is the smart thing to do. God's commandments are not burdensome obligations but pathways to a joyful, meaningful, satisfying life. God's call for your obedience is based on his own commitment to your well-being. Since God is the creator of life, he knows how life is supposed to work. Even though his commandments are sometimes difficult or don't seem to make sense from a human perspective, obedience to him will always bring blessing, joy, and peace. Obedience demonstrates your willingness and trust to follow through on what God says is best for you. Obedience is the visible expression of your love. Disobedience is not so much about breaking a law as it is about breaking God's heart.

Divine Promise

THE LORD WILL WITHHOLD NO GOOD THING FROM THOSE WHO DO WHAT IS RIGHT.

Psalm 84:11

Opportunities

My Question *for* God

How do I make the most of opportunities that come my way?

A Moment *with* God

Two full years later . . . Pharaoh sent for Joseph at once, and he was quickly brought from the prison. . . . Then Pharaoh said to Joseph, "Since God has revealed the meaning of the dreams to you, clearly no one else is as intelligent or wise as you are. You will be in charge of my court, and all my people will take orders from you. Only I, sitting on my throne, will have a rank higher than yours."   Genesis 41:1, 14, 39-40

Make the most of every opportunity in these evil days.   Ephesians 5:16

Responsibility opens the doors of opportunity. How you handle each responsibility determines whether or not you will be trusted with more. Joseph was unjustly thrown into prison. He could have whined and complained, become bitter, and done nothing. Instead, he seized every opportunity he could in his situation, quickly earned others' trust because of his responsibility, and eventually rose to great prominence in Egypt. When you see an opportunity to do good, jump on it. The more you think about it, the less likely you are to act. Good deeds should be a natural reflex of obedient faith. God regularly places "divine moments" right in front of you—opportunities to do good, to help someone in need, or to share what you know about God. Always be on the lookout for these opportunities to be a witness for your faith in word or deed. God will put them in front of you; you need to act on them.

DIVINE PROMISE

I KNOW ALL THE THINGS YOU DO, AND I HAVE OPENED A DOOR FOR YOU THAT NO ONE CAN CLOSE. *Revelation 3:8*

Oppression

MY QUESTION *for* GOD

Where does spiritual oppression come from, and how does God help me fight it?

A MOMENT *with* GOD

The world offers only a craving for physical pleasure, a craving for everything we see, and pride in our achievements and possessions. These are not from the Father, but are from this world.   1 JOHN 2:16

Don't be afraid, for I am with you. Don't be discouraged, for I am your God. I will strengthen you
and help you. I will hold you up with my victorious
right hand.

ISAIAH 41:10

Put on all of God's armor so that you will be able to
stand firm against all strategies of the devil.

EPHESIANS 6:11

When Satan has targeted you for attack, you are spiritually oppressed. To defeat you, he focuses on your
weak spots, those areas you refuse to give over to God's
control. The areas in which you compromise your convictions are joints in your spiritual armor at which the
evil one takes aim. You cannot fight Satan alone. You
must use the armor God has given you. You must resist
and fight, for you are in the middle of spiritual warfare,
and the battle is over your very soul. So you must use
every weapon God provides for you. Remember that
God is a warrior. He is always ready to fight on your
behalf, always ready to come to your defense. Join God
in the battle; if you do not, you will be vulnerable and
helpless to withstand the enemy. If you join, you are
guaranteed victory.

DIVINE PROMISE

HE WILL RESCUE YOU. . . . HE WILL KEEP YOU
FROM EVIL. *Job 5:19*

Overcoming

MY QUESTION for GOD

How do I overcome obstacles in my life?

A MOMENT with GOD

On October 2 the wall was finished—just fifty-two days after we had begun. When our enemies and the surrounding nations heard about it, they were frightened and humiliated. They realized this work had been done with the help of our God.

NEHEMIAH 6:15-16

Each time [the Lord] said, "My grace is all you need. My power works best in weakness." So now I am glad to boast about my weaknesses, so that the power of Christ can work through me. That's why I take pleasure in my weaknesses, and in the insults, hardships, persecutions, and troubles that I suffer for Christ. For when I am weak, then I am strong.

2 CORINTHIANS 12:9-10

Just as the Israelites faced the urgent task of building a wall around their city in a very short time, you may also be facing some task or obstacle that seems impossible. The challenge to "build the wall" is met by courageous obedience to what God calls you to do one day at a time. You may think you can't do the big work God has planned for you, but you can do the little tasks he asks you to do today—you can put one brick on top of the other. Then you trust God to do what you can't do. You do your part, and he'll do the rest. That's all he asks. Then the big task gets done. When you begin to see the obstacles in your life as opportunities for God to show his power, they will not seem so overwhelming. The very hardships and weaknesses that frighten you are the same things that strengthen your faith and make your task important. When you are looking at any obstacle, there is always something you can do: a brick to lay, a phone call to make, a note to write, anything. In taking those small steps of obedience each day, you will find you have been building a great work for God, one brick at a time.

DIVINE PROMISE

BECAUSE THE SOVEREIGN LORD HELPS ME, I WILL NOT BE DISGRACED. THEREFORE, I HAVE SET MY FACE LIKE A STONE, DETERMINED TO DO HIS WILL. AND I KNOW THAT I WILL NOT BE PUT TO SHAME. *Isaiah 50:7*

Pain

MY QUESTION *for* GOD

What hope do I have for living through painful circumstances?

A MOMENT *with* GOD

After you have suffered a little while, he will restore, support, and strengthen you, and he will place you on a firm foundation.   1 PETER 5:10

We believers also groan, even though we have the
Holy Spirit within us as a foretaste of future glory,
for we long for our bodies to be released from sin and
suffering. We, too, wait with eager hope for the day
when God will give us our full rights as his adopted
children, including the new bodies he has promised
us. We were given this hope when we were saved. (If
we already have something, we don't need to hope for
it. But if we look forward to something we don't yet
have, we must wait patiently and confidently.)

ROMANS 8:23-25

From betrayal, neglect, and abandonment to breaking an arm or developing a serious illness, the result
is emotional or physical pain. When you look back on
your life, you probably remember times of physical tension from your aching body, or the chest-tightening
ache that comes from a broken heart. Your greatest
hope in times of pain is finding healing from God. He
doesn't take the day off and forget about you. When
you accidentally cut yourself, you become completely
focused on how bad it is and on how to stop the bleed-
ing. When you feel God has abandoned you, it might
be because you have become so focused on easing the
pain of your problems that you have neglected God and
forgotten that he has promised to help you in your difficulties. To abandon you, God would have to stop loving you, and he cannot do that, for he *is* love. Although
he does not promise to remove your pain, God does
promise to be with you in it and to give you hope and
purpose in the despair of your aching body and soul.

Most important, God promises to remove your pain forever in eternity.

DIVINE PROMISE

WHAT WE SUFFER NOW IS NOTHING COMPARED TO THE GLORY HE WILL REVEAL TO US LATER. *Romans 8:18*

Panic

MY QUESTION *for* GOD

How can I keep from panicking when my life seems to be falling apart?

A MOMENT *with* GOD

Troubles surround me—too many to count! My sins pile up so high I can't see my way out. They outnumber the hairs on my head. I have lost all courage.   PSALM 40:12

Fear and trembling overwhelm me, and I can't stop shaking.   PSALM 55:5

Wherever there is jealousy and selfish ambition, there you will find disorder and evil of every kind.

JAMES 3:16

It's your sins that have cut you off from God. Because of your sins, he has turned away and will not listen anymore.   ISAIAH 59:2

With the Lord's authority I say this: Live no longer as the Gentiles do, for they are hopelessly confused.

EPHESIANS 4:17

Panic is physically and emotionally paralyzing—it is where worry and fear meet in an instant crisis. If you aren't prepared for it, you will be too frozen to deal with it properly. Good preparation expels fear, gives you peace about the future, and provides daily confidence to anticipate problems and deal with an instant crisis. The best preparation for crisis (which brings panic) is gaining wisdom through a daily obedient walk with God. Disobeying God can leave you vulnerable to situations that cause panic. In fact, disobedience to God can sometimes actually cause those situations. Each act of rebellion cuts at the lifeline of God's safety and protection. Although a crisis can arise even when you are obeying God, the closer you are to him, the more you can tap into his courage and peace when panic strikes, and the wiser you will be to deal with it. Then you will have a clear head and the wisdom to respond with courage and grace. Ultimately, a life without God causes more panic, because you can't see a purpose to your problems or a future beyond this life. When you believe that God is in control of your life, you know he holds it together. Then, when one or two pieces fall out of place, you will not panic that your whole life is falling apart.

THE LORD YOUR GOD IS LIVING AMONG
YOU. HE IS A MIGHTY SAVIOR. HE WILL TAKE
DELIGHT IN YOU WITH GLADNESS. WITH HIS
LOVE, HE WILL CALM ALL YOUR FEARS. HE WILL
REJOICE OVER YOU WITH JOYFUL SONGS.

Zephaniah 3:17

Passion

MY QUESTION *for* GOD

What inspires passion for God?

A MOMENT *with* GOD

Yours, O LORD, is the greatness, the power, the
glory, the victory, and the majesty. Everything in the
heavens and on earth is yours, O LORD, and this is
your kingdom. We adore you as the one who is over
all things.   1 CHRONICLES 29:11

A clear understanding of who God is makes for passionate worship. The more you learn about God, the
more your heart will naturally long to praise him.

Like newborn babies, you must crave pure spiritual
milk so that you will grow into a full experience of
salvation. Cry out for this nourishment, now that you
have had a taste of the Lord's kindness.   1 PETER 2:2-3

*R*eading God's Word creates a hunger for spiritual growth. The more you grow, the more passionate you'll be about God and about maturing in your faith.

God knows how often I pray for you. Day and night I bring you and your needs in prayer to God, whom I serve with all my heart by spreading the Good News about his Son.   ROMANS 1:9

*I*t is often through prayer that God reveals his desires for your life. As you talk with God and align your mind with his, his desires become your deepest passions.

When they came to the other side, Elijah said to Elisha, "Tell me what I can do for you before I am taken away." And Elisha replied, "Please let me inherit a double share of your spirit and become your successor."   2 KINGS 2:9

*O*ther people can inspire a passion for God in you. A godly mentor, teacher, or friend can open your eyes to the wonderful blessings of serving God and walking in his ways. Elijah was Elisha's mentor. As Elisha watched and learned from the great prophet, he was inspired to become Elijah's successor and an even greater prophet. Likewise, perhaps your walk with God can inspire others to pursue God and serve him even more passionately.

We have heard of your faith in Christ Jesus and your love for all of God's people, which come from your confident hope of what God has reserved for you in heaven. You have had this expectation ever since you first heard the truth of the Good News.

COLOSSIANS 1:4-5

*A*n eternal perspective on life brings passionate action on earth. What you do today has an impact in eternity, which should inspire you to live faithfully and with great fervor to serve the Lord.

DIVINE PROMISE

THE LORD YOUR GOD WILL CHANGE YOUR HEART AND THE HEARTS OF ALL YOUR DESCENDANTS, SO THAT YOU WILL LOVE HIM WITH ALL YOUR HEART AND SOUL AND SO YOU MAY LIVE! *Deuteronomy 30:6*

Past

MY QUESTION *for* GOD

What can help me remember God's work in my past?

A MOMENT *with* GOD

Watch out! Be careful never to forget what you yourself have seen. Do not let these memories escape from your mind as long as you live! And be sure to pass them on to your children and grandchildren.

DEUTERONOMY 4:9

Remember the things I have done in the past. For I alone am God! I am God, and there is none like me.

ISAIAH 46:9

Don't let the excitement of youth cause you to forget your Creator. Honor him in your youth before you grow old and say, "Life is not pleasant anymore."

ECCLESIASTES 12:1

Beware that in your plenty you do not forget the LORD your God and disobey his commands, regulations, and decrees.   DEUTERONOMY 8:11

Let all that I am praise the LORD; may I never forget the good things he does for me.   PSALM 103:2

*I*t is easy to forget what you value least. When you make sure that God remains your top priority, you will be more likely to remember his work in your life. You can do this by telling others about what God has done by meditating on his work in your life, by reading his Word to remember how God has worked in history, and by enjoying and sharing his blessings with future generations. When you do these things, you help yourself and others to remember God's work in the past and to find hope for the future.

DIVINE PROMISE

HE CAUSES US TO REMEMBER HIS WONDERFUL WORKS. HOW GRACIOUS AND MERCIFUL IS OUR LORD! *Psalm 111:4*

Patience

MY QUESTION *for* GOD

How can I develop patience in my busy life?

A MOMENT *with* GOD

Because of [God's] glory and excellence, he has
given us great and precious promises. These are the
promises that enable you to share his divine nature
and escape the world's corruption caused by human
desires. In view of all this, make every effort to
respond to God's promises. Supplement your faith
with a generous provision of moral excellence, and
moral excellence with knowledge, and knowledge
with self-control, and self-control with patient
endurance, and patient endurance with godliness,
and godliness with brotherly affection, and brotherly
affection with love for everyone.   2 PETER 1:4-7

Consider the farmers who patiently wait for the rains
in the fall and in the spring. They eagerly look for the
valuable harvest to ripen.   JAMES 5:7

We were given this hope when we were saved. (If we
already have something, we don't need to hope for
it. But if we look forward to something we don't yet
have, we must wait patiently and confidently.)

ROMANS 8:24-25

Contrary to popular opinion, patience is not merely a
personality trait. Patience is a by-product of the pres-

ence and work of God in your heart, helping you to endure and persevere through frustrating circumstances with grace and self-control. Goals are rarely achieved by quantum leaps but rather by small steps. Patience comes from taking small faithful steps toward your goals and holding on to hope when circumstances block your way. Whether you're waiting for crops to ripen, a traffic jam to unsnarl, a child to mature, or God to perfect you, you can grow in patience by recognizing that this process takes time and that there is only so much you can do to speed it up. In fact, it is only through persevering in and enduring frustrating circumstances that you will develop patience. When you're going through hard times, the hope you have in God's plans for your life—especially his eternal plans—can help you take the faithful steps that will bring you to the other side. When you know that your eternal future is secure, you can grow in patience through today's frustrations.

DIVINE PROMISE

PUT YOUR HOPE IN THE LORD. TRAVEL STEADILY ALONG HIS PATH. HE WILL HONOR YOU.
Psalm 37:34

Peace

MY QUESTION *for* GOD

How can I find peace?

A MOMENT *with* GOD

Don't worry about anything; instead, pray about
everything. Tell God what you need, and thank him
for all he has done. Then you will experience God's
peace, which exceeds anything we can understand.
His peace will guard your hearts and minds as you
live in Christ Jesus.   PHILIPPIANS 4:6-7

The Holy Spirit produces this kind of fruit in our
lives . . . peace.   GALATIANS 5:22

You will keep in perfect peace all who trust in you,
all whose thoughts are fixed on you!   ISAIAH 26:3

Ironically, inner peace doesn't come from you. It
comes only from God, the source of peace. Those
who believe in God have the Holy Spirit, God's promised presence, living within them. God's Spirit brings
peace of mind and heart when you give up control of
your life. Peace of mind comes as God guides you into
his purpose for your life and helps you see life from
his perspective, not from your human one. Peace of
heart comes as God's Spirit guides you into productive living and comforts you in times of trouble. When
you are secure in your eternal purpose and are living with a clear conscience, you will have confidence
that God is watching over you and empowering you
with his strength, protecting you from spiritual danger, and surrounding you with encouragement. When
your life starts to spin out of control, prayer becomes
your gateway to peace. Your spirit will lighten as you

unburden your soul to God. His peace is like a guard on patrol, protecting you from assaults of anxiety or concern. Your problems will always control you when you are focused solely on them. Instead, turn your eyes from your problems, and let yourself be impassioned by the bigger purposes of God. Then you can experience peace despite your problems.

DIVINE PROMISE

MAY THE LORD OF PEACE HIMSELF GIVE YOU HIS PEACE AT ALL TIMES AND IN EVERY SITUATION.   *2 Thessalonians 3:16*

Persecution

MY QUESTION *for* GOD

Why is it so important to endure persecution rather than give in to it?

A MOMENT *with* GOD

I take pleasure in my weaknesses, and in the insults, hardships, persecutions, and troubles that I suffer for Christ. For when I am weak, then I am strong.

2 CORINTHIANS 12:10

We can rejoice, too, when we run into problems and trials, for we know that they help us develop endurance. And endurance develops strength of

character, and character strengthens our confident
hope of salvation.   ROMANS 5:3-4

God's heroes are those who hang on to their faith
in him no matter what happens. For your faith to be
strong and genuine, you need to endure testing. Sometimes the hardest test to endure is being scorned,
mocked, or ignored by others because of your faith in
God. It is during these hard times that your character
is stretched and your real self is exposed. How you
handle persecution shows who you really are on the
inside and defines your level of commitment to God.
By enduring persecution, you show that your faith and
trust in God are honest and real. The Bible is full of
examples of people who never stopped trusting God,
even though they were mocked, persecuted, and even
killed for their faith. God may not ask you to be a mar-
tyr for him, but is your faith strong enough to endure
even a little derision or scorn? Those who live boldly
for God despite opposition will make the greatest impact for eternity.

DIVINE PROMISE

THE MORE WE SUFFER FOR CHRIST, THE MORE
GOD WILL SHOWER US WITH HIS COMFORT
THROUGH CHRIST.   *2 Corinthians 1:5*

Perseverance

MY QUESTION *for* GOD

How can I develop perseverance?

A MOMENT *with* GOD

Then the way you live will always honor and please the Lord, and your lives will produce every kind of good fruit. All the while, you will grow as you learn to know God better and better. We also pray that you will be strengthened with all his glorious power so you will have all the endurance and patience you need. May you be filled with joy.　　COLOSSIANS 1:10-11

Dear brothers and sisters, when troubles come your way, consider it an opportunity for great joy. For you know that when your faith is tested, your endurance has a chance to grow. So let it grow, for when your endurance is fully developed, you will be perfect and complete, needing nothing.　　JAMES 1:2-4

*P*roblems, trials, troubles, and the testing of your faith can either strengthen your resolve or break you down. It all depends on your attitude. If you see your problems as stepping stones to becoming stronger, you can move ahead with anticipation for what you will become—a person of solid character who can handle any obstacle. If you see your problems as giant barriers, you will get discouraged, give up, turn back, and never allow yourself to become more than you are now. Perseverance is based on the promise of God's persistent, faithful work in your life. God never stops working in you, and that should motivate you to always be looking for what he will do next to help you grow. The fuel of endurance for life is the power of God working in you. The more obedient and in tune you are with God, the more God's power will strengthen and ignite your ability to keep on keeping on—not just to endure but to persevere joyfully!

DIVINE PROMISE

IF WE ARE FAITHFUL TO THE END, TRUSTING GOD JUST AS FIRMLY AS WHEN WE FIRST BELIEVED, WE WILL SHARE IN ALL THAT BELONGS TO CHRIST.   *Hebrews 3:14*

Place

MY QUESTIONS *for* GOD

Why are certain places so special to me? Why do I feel closer to God in some places?

A MOMENT *with* GOD

The LORD took hold of me and said, "Get up and go out into the valley, and I will speak to you there." So I got up and went, and there I saw the glory of the LORD, just as I had seen in my first vision by the Kebar River. And I fell face down on the ground.

EZEKIEL 3:22-23

You came down at Mount Sinai and spoke to
them from heaven. You gave them regulations
and instructions that were just, and decrees and
commands that were good.   NEHEMIAH 9:13

*P*laces where you feel closer to God become special
places for you. Ezekiel experienced the glory of God
in a valley. God spoke to the Israelites at Mount Sinai.
Perhaps for you that special place is a local park bench
or even your living-room chair. When you encounter
God, that place reminds you of that moment of closeness with God and makes it forever special.

The LORD God said, "It is not good for the man to be
alone. I will make a helper who is just right for him."
                                            GENESIS 2:18

Where two or three gather together as my followers,
I am there among them.   MATTHEW 18:20

*P*eople make places special. The Garden of Eden
was a beautiful home for Adam. Yet God noticed that
something was missing, something that would complete Eden as the perfect home for Adam: a human
relationship. Do you have special family-vacation spots
or a favorite place to meet friends? These places become special because of the people who are with you
there. Where believers meet, you can often feel God's
presence more keenly.

My people will live in safety, quietly at home. They
will be at rest.   ISAIAH 32:18

$\mathcal{P}$laces of rest can become special because you are able to find a break from the busyness of life and focus more intently on God. Anyplace you can get a break from busy schedules, meetings, and other stresses of life is special because it refreshes your body and soul. Your home should be one of these places, not only for you but also for others to find refuge.

You must call a meeting of the church. I will be present with you in spirit, and so will the power of our Lord Jesus.   1 CORINTHIANS 5:4

When they arrived in Jerusalem, Barnabas and Paul were welcomed by the whole church, including the apostles and elders. They reported everything God had done through them.   ACTS 15:4

$\mathcal{C}$hurch is a special place where you can be part of a group of people who share a common faith in God, where you feel welcome and a sense of belonging with other members of God's family. Church is also meant to be a place to worship, to share, and to serve. The special nature of church is best summed up in the phrase *church home* or *church family*.

I saw a new heaven and a new earth, for the old heaven and the old earth had disappeared. And the sea was also gone. And I saw the holy city, the new Jerusalem, coming down from God out of heaven like a bride beautifully dressed for her husband. I heard a loud shout from the throne, saying, "Look, God's home is now among his people! He will live with them, and they will be his people. God himself will be with them. He will wipe every tear from their eyes, and there will be no more death or sorrow or crying or pain. All these things are gone forever.

REVELATION 21:1-4

*M*any places are special because they offer glimpses of your eternal home in heaven. The glory of the old Jerusalem was a glimpse of the new Jerusalem in heaven. The beauty of this earth, genuine love between friends or family members, and places of rest and renewal are all tastes of heavenly beauty, love, and joy.

DIVINE PROMISE

DON'T LET YOUR HEARTS BE TROUBLED. TRUST IN GOD, AND TRUST ALSO IN ME. THERE IS MORE THAN ENOUGH ROOM IN MY FATHER'S HOME. IF THIS WERE NOT SO, WOULD I HAVE TOLD YOU THAT I AM GOING TO PREPARE A PLACE FOR YOU? WHEN EVERYTHING IS READY, I WILL COME AND GET YOU, SO THAT YOU WILL ALWAYS BE WITH ME WHERE I AM. AND YOU KNOW THE WAY TO WHERE I AM GOING.

John 14:1-4

Potential

MY QUESTION *for* GOD

How can I realize my potential?

A MOMENT *with* GOD

You are the salt of the earth. But what good is salt if it has lost its flavor? Can you make it salty again? It will be thrown out and trampled underfoot as worthless. You are the light of the world—like a city on a hilltop that cannot be hidden. No one lights a lamp and then puts it under a basket. Instead, a lamp is placed on a stand, where it gives light to everyone in the house. In the same way, let your good deeds shine out for all to see, so that everyone will praise your heavenly Father.

MATTHEW 5:13-16

*H*ow often have you searched drawers and closets for a flashlight, only to discover, when you finally find it, that the batteries are dead? Although the flashlight has the potential to provide light, without fresh batteries it is useless. You have within you the light of God and therefore, the potential to shine on others in a way that draws them to him. But if you lose your light, cover your light, or fail to allow the power of the Holy Spirit to illumine your heart, you are like a dead flashlight. Within yourself you don't have the power to reach your full potential. Only by God's power working in you can you reach your fullest potential.

DIVINE PROMISE

I PRAY THAT YOUR HEARTS WILL BE FLOODED
WITH LIGHT SO THAT YOU CAN UNDERSTAND
THE CONFIDENT HOPE HE HAS GIVEN TO

THOSE HE CALLED—HIS HOLY PEOPLE WHO ARE
HIS RICH AND GLORIOUS INHERITANCE.
Ephesians 1:18

Power of God

MY QUESTION *for* GOD

How can I experience God's power working through me?

A MOMENT *with* GOD

Each time [the Lord] said, "My grace is all you need.
My power works best in weakness." So now I am glad
to boast about my weaknesses, so that the power of
Christ can work through me.   2 CORINTHIANS 12:9

This is the secret: Christ lives in you. This gives you
assurance of sharing his glory. . . . That's why I work
and struggle so hard, depending on Christ's mighty
power that works within me.   COLOSSIANS 1:27-29

Be strong in the Lord and in his mighty power. Put
on all of God's armor so that you will be able to stand
firm against all strategies of the devil. For we are not
fighting against flesh-and-blood enemies, but against
evil rulers and authorities of the unseen world,
against mighty powers in this dark world, and against
evil spirits in the heavenly places.   EPHESIANS 6:10-12

It seems logical that only a strong person would
have the capacity to experience the power of God. But

the truth is, God's power is not dependent on human strength. In fact, God's power is most evident when you are weak, because then it is only by God's strength that you are able to accomplish what you cannot do on your own. Your strength or power comes from God's presence within you. You do not merely imitate him or try through your own efforts to do right and please God. You have his Holy Spirit, with his power, working in you. When opposition or problems arise, try not to look at the size of the problem but at the size of your God. When there are great things to be done, you have a great God who is able to do them through you.

DIVINE PROMISE

WITH GOD'S HELP WE WILL DO
MIGHTY THINGS.   *Psalm 60:12*

Practice

MY QUESTION *for* GOD

Why is it important to practice spiritual virtues and disciplines?

A MOMENT *with* GOD

Joseph was a very handsome and well-built young man, and Potiphar's wife soon began to look at him lustfully. "Come and sleep with me," she demanded. . . . She kept putting pressure on Joseph day after day, but he refused to sleep with her, and he kept out of her way as much as possible. One day . . . she came and grabbed him by his cloak, demanding, "Come on, sleep with me!" Joseph tore himself away, but he left his cloak in her hand as he ran from the house.

GENESIS 39:6-7, 10-12

Give me understanding and I will obey your instructions; I will put them into practice with all my heart.   PSALM 119:34

Let us stop going over the basic teachings about Christ again and again. Let us go on instead and become mature in our understanding. Surely we don't need to start again with the fundamental importance of repenting from evil deeds and placing our faith in God. You don't need further instruction about baptisms, the laying on of hands, the resurrection of the dead, and eternal judgment. And so, God willing, we will move forward to further understanding.   HEBREWS 6:1-3

The old expression practice makes perfect is only half true. *Accurate* practice makes perfect. Practice is more than avoiding mistakes; it is also learning to strive for excellence. For example, when you are learning to play an instrument, avoiding mistakes is basic; but to be truly musical, you have to learn to play the correct notes with proper rhythm, volume, and feeling. The same is true when you are practicing spiritual disciplines. Avoiding mistakes, or sin, is basic. The next step is to begin living with virtue and discipline, practicing daily until they become second nature—God's nature. The more you practice the disciplines of godly character—daily Bible study, prayer, meditation, and service—the more you resemble Jesus and live with integrity and purity.

DIVINE PROMISE

KEEP PUTTING INTO PRACTICE ALL YOU LEARNED AND RECEIVED FROM ME— EVERYTHING YOU HEARD FROM ME AND SAW ME DOING. THEN THE GOD OF PEACE WILL BE WITH YOU.   *Philippians 4:9*

Praise

MY QUESTION *for* GOD

How can I be inspired to praise God?

A MOMENT *with* GOD

As he rode along, the crowds spread out their garments on the road ahead of him. When he reached the place where the road started down the Mount of Olives, all of his followers began to shout and sing as they walked along, praising God for all the wonderful miracles they had seen.   LUKE 19:36-37

Great is the LORD! He is most worthy of praise! He is to be feared above all gods. The gods of other nations are mere idols, but the LORD made the heavens!

1 CHRONICLES 16:25-26

$\mathcal{I}$t is not unusual for observers to burst into spontaneous applause or cheers when a celebrity enters a room. This is a natural response to the presence of a person of power, position, or accomplishment. Likewise, when you enter the presence of God in worship, your natural response should be praise and adoration. The Bible teaches that God is the creator of the universe: He fashioned the heavens, placed the planets and stars in motion, carved out the canyons and valleys and mountains, and breathed life into every human being; and he desires a personal relationship with us and even provides a way for us to live forever with him in heaven. As the creator and sustainer of life, he is worthy of our highest praise. Perhaps the best way to realize the awesome power and presence of God is to consider his greatness compared with your mortality and weakness. As you consider his unlimited and unconditional love for you personally, despite your limitations, you will begin to find yourself responding to him with more adoration, joy, and praise.

DIVINE PROMISE

WHEN [CHRIST] COMES ON THAT DAY, HE WILL RECEIVE GLORY FROM HIS HOLY PEOPLE— PRAISE FROM ALL WHO BELIEVE. AND THIS INCLUDES YOU, FOR YOU BELIEVED WHAT WE TOLD YOU ABOUT HIM.   *2 Thessalonians 1:10*

Prayer

MY QUESTION *for* GOD

How can I know God hears my prayers?

A MOMENT *with* GOD

We are confident that he hears us whenever we ask
for anything that pleases him.   1 JOHN 5:14

Keep on asking, and you will receive what you ask
for. Keep on seeking, and you will find. Keep on
knocking, and the door will be opened to you. For
everyone who asks, receives. Everyone who seeks,
finds. And to everyone who knocks, the door will be
opened. You parents—if your children ask for a loaf
of bread, do you give them a stone instead? Or if they
ask for a fish, do you give them a snake? Of course
not! So if you sinful people know how to give good
gifts to your children, how much more will your
heavenly Father give good gifts to those who ask him.

                                                  MATTHEW 7:7-11

$\mathscr{S}$ometimes your growth through prayer is the best
evidence that God is listening to your prayers. There is
so much more to prayer than just getting an answer to
a question or a solution for a problem. God often does
more in your heart through the act of prayer than he
does in actually answering your prayer. As you persist
in conversation with God, you will gain greater understanding of yourself, your situation, your motivation,
and God's nature and direction for your life. You won't

always get the specific answer you are looking for, but you will receive better things: the power and desire to obey God, the strength to overcome evil with good, the supernatural ability to love and forgive, the character to persevere in your faith, and the courage to be his witness to those who don't know him. You can pray confidently for wisdom and guidance in all situations, knowing that you are asking for the very things he most longs to give.

DIVINE PROMISE

THE LORD IS CLOSE TO ALL WHO CALL ON HIM, YES, TO ALL WHO CALL ON HIM IN TRUTH.

Psalm 145:18

Presence of God

MY QUESTION *for* GOD

How can I experience God's presence in my life?

A MOMENT *with* GOD

If my people . . . will humble themselves and pray and seek my face and turn from their wicked ways, I will hear from heaven and will forgive their sins.

2 CHRONICLES 7:14

Come close to God, and God will come close to you.
Wash your hands, you sinners; purify your hearts, for
your loyalty is divided between God and the world.

JAMES 4:8

When you pray, I will listen. If you look for me
wholeheartedly, you will find me.   JEREMIAH 29:12-13

God is working in you, giving you the desire and the
power to do what pleases him.   PHILIPPIANS 2:13

I know the LORD is always with me. I will not be
shaken, for he is right beside me. No wonder my
heart is glad, and I rejoice. My body rests in safety.
. . . You will show me the way of life, granting me
the joy of your presence and the pleasures of living
with you forever.   PSALM 16:8-11

You have shown me the way of life, and you will fill
me with the joy of your presence.   ACTS 2:28

One of the most awesome and mind-boggling charac-
teristics of God is that he is omnipresent—he is everywhere at all times. Since God is already present with
you, it's up to you to draw near to him to experience
closeness with him. God promises that when you truly
look for him, you will find him. The best way is to start
talking with him through prayer, confessing your sins,
asking for guidance, and promising him you will become
aware of his presence in new and wonderful ways.

DIVINE PROMISE

THE SPIRIT IS GOD'S GUARANTEE THAT HE
WILL GIVE US THE INHERITANCE HE PROMISED
AND THAT HE HAS PURCHASED US TO BE HIS
OWN PEOPLE. HE DID THIS SO WE WOULD
PRAISE AND GLORIFY HIM.   *Ephesians 1:14*

Pressure

MY QUESTION *for* GOD

How can I best deal with the pressures of life?

A MOMENT *with* GOD

Martha was distracted by the big dinner she was
preparing. She came to Jesus and said, "Lord, doesn't
it seem unfair to you that my sister just sits here while
I do all the work? Tell her to come and help me."
But the Lord said to her, "My dear Martha, you are
worried and upset over all these details!"   LUKE 10:40-41

As pressure and stress bear down on me, I find joy in
your commands.   PSALM 119:143

"This is not good!" Moses' father-in-law exclaimed.
"You're going to wear yourself out—and the people,
too. This job is too heavy a burden for you to handle
all by yourself."   EXODUS 18:17-18

Pressure can cause you to focus on the trivial and miss
the significant. As pressure squeezes your perspective

inward, you lose your ability to look outward. Preoccupation with the constant urgency of the moment blinds you to the big picture. What can you do when you're feeling pressure? First, try turning your thoughts away from the insignificant, and focus on what's most important to God, not what's important to you. When you think about all God is doing rather than about what you should be doing, the pressures of life can seem less urgent. Second, immerse yourself in and obey God's Word, where you will find the secrets to lasting joy. The more you find joy in God, the less you will feel stress from external pressures. Finally, allow others to help you with the load. No one ever said you have to do it all yourself, and the solution of accepting help from others is often overlooked. When the pressures of life weigh you down, you can respond with wisdom from God's Word, an eternal perspective, and a little more help from your friends.

DIVINE PROMISE

JESUS SAID, "COME TO ME, ALL OF YOU WHO
ARE WEARY AND CARRY HEAVY BURDENS,
AND I WILL GIVE YOU REST. TAKE MY YOKE
UPON YOU. LET ME TEACH YOU, BECAUSE I
AM HUMBLE AND GENTLE AT HEART, AND
YOU WILL FIND REST FOR YOUR SOULS. FOR
MY YOKE IS EASY TO BEAR, AND THE BURDEN
I GIVE YOU IS LIGHT." *Matthew 11:28-30*

Problems

MY QUESTION *for* GOD

What do I do when problems overwhelm me?

A MOMENT *with* GOD

Dear brothers and sisters, when troubles come your way, consider it an opportunity for great joy.   JAMES 1:2

The LORD helps the fallen and lifts those bent beneath their loads.   PSALM 145:14

Why am I discouraged? Why is my heart so sad? I will put my hope in God! I will praise him again—my Savior and my God! Now I am deeply discouraged, but I will remember you.   PSALM 42:5-6

*O*verwhelming problems are opportunities to experience God's help. When problems arise unexpectedly, they can cause you to become discouraged, to lose hope, to feel sorry for yourself, or to forget God's promises to you. At those times it's helpful to remember God's past faithfulness, which helps you trust him today and gives you the hope you need to help you face your problems tomorrow. Recalling what God has done for you ignites the fire of hope, and praise drives away the darkness of despair that causes self-pity. You must be willing to look away from yourself long enough to see God's hand reaching out to help you. God finds you when you've fallen and never passes you by, but you have to want to be helped up. Indulging in self-pity or wanting to control the situation all by yourself contributes only to the overwhelming burden of your problems. When you feel you can't go another step, allow God to shoulder your load, ease your burden, and heal your pain.

DIVINE PROMISE

JOYFUL ARE THOSE WHO HAVE THE GOD OF ISRAEL AS THEIR HELPER, WHOSE HOPE IS IN THE LORD THEIR GOD.   *Psalm 146:5*

Promises of God

MY QUESTION *for* GOD

What are some of the great promises of God?

A MOMENT *with* GOD

God loved the world so much that he gave his one and only Son, so that everyone who believes in him will not perish but have eternal life.   JOHN 3:16

The wages of sin is death, but the free gift of God is eternal life through Christ Jesus our Lord.   ROMANS 6:23

God promises salvation to all who accept it. Those who believe that Jesus died for their sins, confess their sins, and are truly sorry for them will be saved from the punishment their sins deserve. God looks at them as if they had never sinned and will give them eternal life in heaven with him.

If you love me, obey my commandments. And I
will ask the Father, and he will give you another
Advocate, who will never leave you. He is the Holy
Spirit, who leads into all truth.   JOHN 14:15-17

God promises to be with you forever in the form of
the Holy Spirit.

Teach these new disciples to obey all the commands
I have given you. And be sure of this: I am with you
always, even to the end of the age.   MATTHEW 28:20

God promises to be with you all the time.

If we confess our sins to him, he is faithful and just
to forgive us our sins and to cleanse us from all
wickedness.   1 JOHN 1:9

God promises to forgive you whenever you do wrong,
if you just ask him. He promises that nothing you do is
beyond his forgiveness.

Don't worry about anything; instead, pray about
everything. Tell God what you need, and thank him
for all he has done. Then you will experience God's
peace, which exceeds anything we can understand.
His peace will guard your hearts and minds as you
live in Christ Jesus.   PHILIPPIANS 4:6-7

*G*od promises you peace of heart and mind when you entrust your life to him.

We know that God causes everything to work together for the good of those who love God and are called according to his purpose for them.   ROMANS 8:28

Our present troubles are small and won't last very long. Yet they produce for us a glory that vastly outweighs them and will last forever!   2 CORINTHIANS 4:17

*G*od promises to use even the bad things that happen to you for good purposes.

The day of the Lord will come as unexpectedly as a thief. Then the heavens will pass away with a terrible noise, and the very elements themselves will disappear in fire, and the earth and everything on it will be found to deserve judgment.   2 PETER 3:10

*G*od promises that Jesus is coming back to judge the world for its deeds.

Our dying bodies must be transformed into bodies that will never die; our mortal bodies must be transformed into immortal bodies.   1 CORINTHIANS 15:53

*G*od promises that all who believe in him—living or dead—will be given new bodies that will never die.

Don't let your hearts be troubled. Trust in God, and trust also in me. There is more than enough room in

my Father's home. If this were not so, would I have
told you that I am going to prepare a place for you?
When everything is ready, I will come and get you, so
that you will always be with me where I am. And you
know the way to where I am going. . . . I am the way,
the truth, and the life. No one can come to the Father
except through me.   JOHN 14:1-6

God promises an eternal home in heaven for those who
trust in Jesus Christ and acknowledge him as Lord.

DIVINE PROMISE

DEEP IN YOUR HEARTS YOU KNOW THAT EVERY
PROMISE OF THE LORD YOUR GOD HAS COME
TRUE. NOT A SINGLE ONE HAS FAILED!
Joshua 23:14

Protection

MY QUESTION *for* GOD

How does God protect me?

A MOMENT *with* GOD

Boaz went over and said to Ruth, "Listen, my daughter.
Stay right here with us when you gather grain; don't go
to any other fields. Stay right behind the young women
working in my field. See which part of the field they
are harvesting, and then follow them. I have warned
the young men not to treat you roughly. And when you

are thirsty, help yourself to the water they have drawn from the well." Ruth fell at his feet and thanked him warmly. "What have I done to deserve such kindness?" she asked. "I am only a foreigner." "Yes, I know," Boaz replied. "But I also know about everything you have done for your mother-in-law since the death of your husband. I have heard how you left your father and mother and your own land to live here among complete strangers. May the LORD, the God of Israel, under whose wings you have come to take refuge, reward you fully for what you have done."   RUTH 2:8-12

It's human nature to think about ourselves first, but that's not God's way. He commands us to think of others first. Too often we worry more about how God is going to protect us, but in the story of Ruth, God makes it clear that he gives us the responsibility of protecting others. If people truly looked out for each other, this world would be a safer and better place. God promises to protect your soul for all eternity if you put your trust in him. But here on earth, most of the protection we get comes when God works through us to watch out for those in need of help. Ruth was vulnerable—a widow in a foreign land with no one to protect her. Fortunately, she chose to glean in a field owned by Boaz, an honorable and godly man. Boaz told Ruth, "I have warned the young men not to treat you roughly" (v. 9). Being a follower of God requires more than knowing what is right. It demands doing what is right. It was Boaz's responsibility not only to watch out for Ruth but also to have the courage to warn the young men who might take advantage of her to stay away. Who do you know who is vulnerable; who needs your help? Is there someone you should look out for? If you don't step in to care for and protect that person, who will? Caring for those who are vulnerable requires courage and conviction. Then you will be the conduit through whom God works to protect others, and others will be the conduit through whom God protects you.

Divine Challenge

FEED THE HUNGRY, AND HELP THOSE IN
TROUBLE. THEN YOUR LIGHT WILL SHINE OUT
FROM THE DARKNESS, AND THE DARKNESS
AROUND YOU WILL BE AS BRIGHT AS NOON.
Isaiah 58:10

Purpose

My Question *for* God

How can I discover God's purpose for my life?

A Moment *with* God

Here now is my final conclusion: Fear God and obey his commands, for this is everyone's duty.

ECCLESIASTES 12:13

My life is worth nothing to me unless I use it for finishing the work assigned me by the Lord Jesus— the work of telling others the Good News about the wonderful grace of God.   ACTS 20:24

A spiritual gift is given to each of us.   1 CORINTHIANS 12:7

Dear brothers and sisters, I plead with you to give
your bodies to God because of all he has done for
you. Let them be a living and holy sacrifice—the
kind he will find acceptable. This is truly the way to
worship him. Don't copy the behavior and customs
of this world, but let God transform you into a new
person by changing the way you think. Then you will
learn to know God's will for you, which is good and
pleasing and perfect.   ROMANS 12:1-2

[Caleb said,] "If the LORD is with me, I will drive
them out of the land, just as the LORD said."

JOSHUA 14:12

God has a general purpose and a specific purpose for
you. You have been chosen by God to let the love of
Jesus shine through you to make an impact on others.
More specifically, God has given you spiritual gifts and
wants you to use them to make a unique contribution
in your sphere of influence. The more you fulfill your
general purpose, the more clear your specific purpose
will become. Discovering God's purpose begins with
your wholehearted commitment to him. You give
yourself to God because he has given himself to you.
God promises to make his will known to you as you
make yourself available to him. He will change you
into a person of purpose if you give God free reign
over your thoughts and actions. God's purpose for you
is best verified by his presence and his participation.
When Caleb realized he was part of God's plan to drive

out the Canaanites, the strength of his enemies was no longer an obstacle. Where is God present and active in your life? Perhaps this will help point you in the direction of God's purpose for you.

Divine Promise

DO NOT TREMBLE; DO NOT BE AFRAID. DID I NOT PROCLAIM MY PURPOSES FOR YOU LONG AGO? YOU ARE MY WITNESSES—IS THERE ANY OTHER GOD? NO! THERE IS NO OTHER ROCK—NOT ONE!   *Isaiah 44:8*

Pursuit by God

My Question *for* God

The Bible says that God is pursuing me. Why would he want to do that?

A Moment *with* God

"I thought to myself, 'I would love to treat you as my own children!' I wanted nothing more than to give you this beautiful land—the finest possession in the world. I looked forward to your calling me 'Father,' and I wanted you never to turn from me." Jeremiah 3:19

"When that day comes," says the Lord . . . "I will show love to those I called 'Not loved.' And to those I called 'Not my people,' I will say, 'Now you are my people.' And they will reply, 'You are our God!'"

Hosea 2:16, 23

I am writing to all of you in Rome who are loved by
God and are called to be his own holy people.

ROMANS 1:7

See how very much our Father loves us, for he calls us
his children, and that is what we are! But the people
who belong to this world don't recognize that we are
God's children because they don't know him.   1 JOHN 3:1

God is looking for a personal relationship with each person he has created. He pursues you not to get something
from you but to give something wonderful to you—help,
hope, power, salvation, joy, peace, and eternal life. He
pursues you because he knows how much these gifts can
transform your life. God's love relentlessly calls everyone to turn away from sin and toward an eternal relationship with him. While his desire is that no one reject
him, he allows the freedom to return his love or to reject
it and spend eternity apart from him and his love. Will
you be captivated by his faithful love? Will the sound of
his voice draw you to him?

DIVINE PROMISE

LONG AGO THE LORD SAID TO ISRAEL:
"I HAVE LOVED YOU, MY PEOPLE, WITH AN
EVERLASTING LOVE. WITH UNFAILING LOVE
I HAVE DRAWN YOU TO MYSELF." *Jeremiah 31:3*

Questions

MY QUESTIONS *for* GOD

Is it wrong to question God's plan and actions in my life?
When I ask him tough questions, will he answer?

A MOMENT *with* GOD

One day Moses said to the LORD, "You have been
telling me, 'Take these people up to the Promised
Land.' But you haven't told me whom you will send
with me. You have told me, 'I know you by name,
and I look favorably on you.' If it is true that you
look favorably on me, let me know your ways so
I may understand you more fully and continue to
enjoy your favor. And remember that this nation is
your very own people." The LORD replied, "I will
personally go with you, Moses, and I will give you
rest—everything will be fine for you."   EXODUS 33:12-14

O LORD, our Rock, you have sent these Babylonians
to correct us, to punish us for our many sins. But
you are pure and cannot stand the sight of evil. Will
you wink at their treachery? Should you be silent
while the wicked swallow up people more righteous
than they?   HABAKKUK 1:12-13

Keep on asking, and you will receive what you ask
for. Keep on seeking, and you will find. Keep on
knocking, and the door will be opened to you.

MATTHEW 7:7

God is patient when you question his plan. Moses was feeling frustrated that God had revealed to him a plan without revealing how that plan would unfold. Moses knew what God had promised, but he became concerned when the fulfillment of those promises took longer than he expected. Despite Moses' impatience, God was patient, reminding Moses that he was with him and that what he had promised would happen, just as he said. When you question God's plan, he doesn't always yield all of the details of how that plan will play out, but he gives you an even better answer: Don't worry about the details, because I am with you. Even when you question and doubt God's actions, you can still remain certain of who he is—faithful and eternal. You can know God is loving and just and still not understand why he allows some things to happen. God welcomes your questions when you don't understand, but he often reveals his faithful character rather than future circumstances. God encourages you to ask him tough questions out of a genuine desire to know and understand him. It is important to ask God the tough questions, because it is in the questions—not the answers—that you find God.

DIVINE PROMISE

IF YOU NEED WISDOM, ASK OUR GENEROUS GOD, AND HE WILL GIVE IT TO YOU. HE WILL NOT REBUKE YOU FOR ASKING. *James 1:5*

Quiet

How important are "quiet times" with God?

A MOMENT *with* GOD

"Go out and stand before me on the mountain," the LORD told him. And as Elijah stood there, the LORD passed by, and a mighty windstorm hit the mountain. It was such a terrible blast that the rocks were torn loose, but the LORD was not in the wind. After the wind there was an earthquake, but the LORD was not in the earthquake. And after the earthquake there was a fire, but the LORD was not in the fire. And after the fire there was the sound of a gentle whisper. When Elijah heard it, he wrapped his face in his cloak and went out and stood at the entrance of the cave.

1 KINGS 19:11-13

Be still, and know that I am God! I will be honored by every nation. I will be honored throughout the world.

PSALM 46:10

When you pray, go away by yourself, shut the door behind you, and pray to your Father in private. Then your Father, who sees everything, will reward you.

MATTHEW 6:6

Most people think of hearing God in the form of a booming voice from heaven. But most often God speaks to people in quiet ways. While you can honor

God during your appointments and tasks of the day, sometimes quiet respect is the best demonstration of your deep reverence. Quiet moments allow for genuine prayer where your conversation with God includes times of just listening. While praying with others is powerful and right, you also need to spend time alone, talking privately with God, where you feel no pressure to pray eloquently or to sound pious. In private, you are free to bare your soul to God and then let him speak to your vulnerability. Finding quiet moments with God is important for learning to distinguish his voice from the other voices competing for your attention. It is often in these times of silence that God whispers to your heart or tugs at your soul. In the busyness of the day, these quiet attempts to get your attention might go unnoticed, but by carving out special times of stillness before God, you will come to know his unique voice. Quiet times are an important part of experiencing God in new ways. Sometimes in a quiet moment with God, he takes hold of your heart and leads you to do his will or gives you an inspirational or visionary thought or the insight to accomplish a special task. It is often in small, quiet moments that God communicates to you big ideas and purposes.

DIVINE PROMISE

THE LORD MUST WAIT FOR YOU TO COME TO HIM SO HE CAN SHOW YOU HIS LOVE AND COMPASSION. FOR THE LORD IS A FAITHFUL GOD. BLESSED ARE THOSE WHO WAIT FOR HIS HELP. *Isaiah 30:18*

Reaching Out

MY QUESTIONS *for* GOD

What is my responsibility to the poor? How much do I need to help those less fortunate than I am?

A MOMENT *with* GOD

When you harvest the crops of your land, do not harvest the grain along the edges of your fields, and do not pick up what the harvesters drop. It is the same with your grape crop—do not strip every last bunch of grapes from the vines, and do not pick up the grapes that fall to the ground. Leave them for the poor and the foreigners living among you. I am the LORD your God.   LEVITICUS 19:9-10

Feed the hungry, and help those in trouble. Then your light will shine out from the darkness, and the darkness around you will be as bright as noon.

ISAIAH 58:10

God has compassion for those in need, so striving for godliness should also include a deep compassion for others. Throughout the Bible, God demonstrates his daily care for the poor. In the verses from Leviticus 19 he instructs farmers to leave some grain and fruit in their fields after harvest so those in need can find food. What can you leave for others from your abundance? Compassion that does not reach into your checkbook or onto your "to do" list is only philosophical, not real compassion. You will not be able to help everyone, but

you are to reach out to those around whom you learn
are needy. Helping the poor and needy is not merely
an obligation; it is a privilege that brings great joy and
blessing from God.

DIVINE PROMISE

IF YOU HELP THE POOR, YOU ARE LENDING TO
THE LORD—AND HE WILL REPAY YOU! *Proverbs 19:17*

Reconciliation

MY QUESTION *for* GOD

Why is reconciliation so important?

A MOMENT *with* GOD

If you are presenting a sacrifice at the altar in the
Temple and you suddenly remember that someone has
something against you, leave your sacrifice there at
the altar. Go and be reconciled to that person. Then
come and offer your sacrifice to God.   MATTHEW 5:23-24

Make allowance for each other's faults, and forgive
anyone who offends you.   COLOSSIANS 3:13

If another believer sins against you, go privately and
point out the offense. If the other person listens and
confesses it, you have won that person back.

MATTHEW 18:15

*R*econciliation is the heart of the story about God and humankind. Ever since sin entered the world, God has been pursuing all people in order to reconcile his relationship with each person. He sent his son, Jesus, to suffer the agony of the cross so that sinful people could be forgiven and therefore reconciled with a holy God. Jesus is saying that our reconciliation with God is to produce reconciliation with others. Reconciliation in human relationships is so important to Jesus that he commands us even to leave worship in order to first be reconciled to the people in our lives with whom we may have conflict. In other words, to live with an unresolved human conflict actually hinders our relationship with God. Some conflict seems impossible to resolve. But being reconciled with other people is important to God because it demonstrates a humble and forgiving spirit, which is essential to healthy relationships. And healthy relationships are what God created us for. Reconciliation becomes possible only when someone makes the first move: a hand extended, a phone call, a word spoken in forgiveness. Is there anyone in your life with whom you need to pursue reconciliation?

DIVINE PROMISE

"MY WAYWARD CHILDREN," SAYS THE LORD, "COME BACK TO ME, AND I WILL HEAL YOUR WAYWARD HEARTS." "YES, WE'RE COMING," THE PEOPLE REPLY, "FOR YOU ARE THE LORD OUR GOD." *Jeremiah 3:22*

Regrets

MY QUESTION *for* GOD

There are a lot of things in my past I regret doing. How can I get over those regrets?

A MOMENT *with* GOD

Peter was sitting outside in the courtyard. A servant girl came over and said to him, "You were one of those with Jesus the Galilean." But Peter denied it in front of everyone. "I don't know what you're talking about," he said. Later, out by the gate, another servant girl noticed him and said to those standing around, "This man was with Jesus of Nazareth." Again Peter denied it, this time with an oath. "I don't even know the man," he said. A little later some of the other bystanders came over to Peter and said, "You must be one of them; we can tell by your Galilean accent." Peter swore, "A curse on me if I'm lying—I don't know the man!" And immediately the rooster crowed. Suddenly, Jesus' words flashed through Peter's mind: "Before the rooster crows, you will deny three times that you even know me." And he went away, weeping bitterly.   MATTHEW 26:69-75

I say to you that you are Peter (which means "rock"), and upon this rock I will build my church, and all the powers of hell will not conquer it.   MATTHEW 16:18

This means that anyone who belongs to Christ has become a new person. The old life is gone; a new life has begun!   2 CORINTHIANS 5:17

If the memories and experiences of your life were compared to rocks collected and carried in a backpack, surely guilt and regret would be among the heaviest of them all. A feeling of guilt is the legitimate spiritual response to sin, while regret is the sorrow over the consequences of your decisions, both the sinful and the simply unfortunate. While God promises to remove the guilt of all who seek his forgiveness, he does not prevent the consequences of sin. It is the regret over those consequences that you often carry, and you become weighed down with remorse. God promises to help you deal with your regrets so that you can move on to the future without carrying a load of guilt. When you come to faith in Jesus, he forgives your sins—all of them. Your past is forgotten to him, and he gives you a fresh start. You will still have to live with the consequences of your sins, because they cannot be retracted. But because God forgives you, you can move forward without the tremendous guilt that can accompany regret. Because God no longer holds your sins against you, you no longer have to hold them against yourself. Now you can be free from self-condemnation. It is a divine moment when you truly grasp the power of God's forgiveness, because then you are able to turn your regrets into resolve. Regrets can be so enslaving that they consume your thoughts and disable you from serving God. If Peter had focused on his regret of denying Jesus, he would never have been able to preach the good news about Jesus so powerfully. Don't let regret paralyze you; instead, let God's forgiveness motivate you to positive action for him in the future.

DIVINE PROMISE

DAVID ALSO SPOKE OF THIS WHEN HE
DESCRIBED THE HAPPINESS OF THOSE WHO
ARE DECLARED RIGHTEOUS WITHOUT
WORKING FOR IT: "OH, WHAT JOY FOR THOSE
WHOSE DISOBEDIENCE IS FORGIVEN, WHOSE
SINS ARE PUT OUT OF SIGHT. YES, WHAT JOY
FOR THOSE WHOSE RECORD THE LORD HAS
CLEARED OF SIN." *Romans 4:6-8*

Rejection

MY QUESTION *for* GOD

Will God ever reject me?

A MOMENT *with* GOD

Jesus replied, "If you only knew the gift God has for
you and who you are speaking to, you would ask me,
and I would give you living water."   JOHN 4:10

*J*esus did not reject the sinful Samaritan woman,
but rather showed her acceptance by offering her living
water. Jesus will never reject anyone who comes to him
to be cleansed from sin.

Jesus stood up again and said to the woman, "Where
are your accusers? Didn't even one of them condemn
you?" "No, Lord," she said. And Jesus said, "Neither
do I. Go and sin no more."   JOHN 8:10-11

*G*od rejects the sin without rejecting the sinner who comes to him.

Those the Father has given me will come to me, and I will never reject them.   JOHN 6:37

*G*od accepts all who come to him in faith, even those who previously rejected him.

Because of Christ and our faith in him, we can now come boldly and confidently into God's presence.

EPHESIANS 3:12

This High Priest of ours understands our weaknesses, for he faced all of the same testings we do, yet he did not sin. So let us come boldly to the throne of our gracious God. There we will receive his mercy, and we will find grace to help us when we need it most.

HEBREWS 4:15-16

*Y*ou can approach God knowing that he gladly welcomes you and will always accept you. God will never say, "Sorry, I don't have time for you" or "I'm busy." He always listens, always hears, always responds, and always loves. Even at your weakest he does not reject you but rather embraces you so that you can receive strength to be all he intends you to be. In his open arms you will find the ultimate example of how to accept others.

Remove your heavy hand from me, and don't terrify me with your awesome presence. Now summon me,

and I will answer! Or let me speak to you, and you
reply. Tell me, what have I done wrong? Show me my
rebellion and my sin. Why do you turn away from me?
Why do you treat me as your enemy?   JOB 13:21-24

Don't misinterpret God's silence as rejection. When
God seems silent, it is usually because you are too busy
to hear him. It might also be that he is being quiet so
that you will draw closer to him in order to more fully
experience his love and acceptance.

DIVINE PROMISE

**THE LORD WILL NOT REJECT HIS PEOPLE; HE
WILL NOT ABANDON HIS SPECIAL POSSESSION.**
Psalm 94:14

Relationships

MY QUESTION *for* GOD

How is God present in my relationships with others?

A MOMENT *with* GOD

Jesus replied, "The most important commandment
is this: 'Listen, O Israel! The LORD our God is the
one and only LORD. And you must love the LORD
your God with all your heart, all your soul, all your
mind, and all your strength.' The second is equally

important: 'Love your neighbor as yourself.' No other commandment is greater than these."

MARK 12:29-31

If we are living in the light, as God is in the light, then we have fellowship with each other, and the blood of Jesus, his Son, cleanses us from all sin.

1 JOHN 1:7

*A*s your relationship with another deepens, you learn to express yourself and your appreciation and commitment to the other. The depth of commitment and ability to communicate often signal the importance of that relationship. Your relationship with God is the most important, although that does not mean that you can or should neglect your relationships with others. It is often through relating to others that you learn more about relating to God. But as you deepen your relationship with God, who made you, you will also learn more about relating to others. God knows how important relationships are, so he has given you the tools and his own Spirit to help you relate effectively to others. Your relationships with others allow you an opportunity to respond with gratitude for God's faithfulness to you. When you love others, you are expressing the love God desires in his relationship with you.

DIVINE PROMISE

NOW WE CAN REJOICE IN OUR WONDERFUL
NEW RELATIONSHIP WITH GOD BECAUSE OUR
LORD JESUS CHRIST HAS MADE US FRIENDS
OF GOD.   *Romans 5:11*

Renewal

MY QUESTION *for* GOD

*My life is a mess and I feel as if I need to start over again.
How can I experience renewal?*

A MOMENT *with* GOD

I will give you a new heart, and I will put a new spirit
in you. I will take out your stony, stubborn heart and
give you a tender, responsive heart.   EZEKIEL 36:26

"Come now, let's settle this," says the LORD. "Though
your sins are like scarlet, I will make them as white as
snow. Though they are red like crimson, I will make
them as white as wool."   ISAIAH 1:18

Since you have heard about Jesus and have learned
the truth that comes from him, throw off your old
sinful nature and your former way of life, which is
corrupted by lust and deception. Instead, let the
Spirit renew your thoughts and attitudes. Put on your
new nature, created to be like God—truly righteous
and holy.   EPHESIANS 4:21-24

Create in me a clean heart, O God. Renew a loyal
spirit within me.   PSALM 51:10

*H*ow often we disappoint ourselves. We have such high hopes and good intentions, but inevitably we find ourselves weary and burned-out with self-defeat, the burdens of everyday living, or the consequences of bad choices and sinful actions. The messiness of life can leave us feeling exhausted, not only physically but also in our very souls. If only we could start over. So many of us are in desperate need of renewal. Renewal begins with the compassion of God and a heart ready for change. When the two are put together, you find a new beginning, a soul refreshed, and a life revived. God makes it clear he will restore any heart that seeks a new start. That new start begins with a sincere desire to turn to God and to turn away from what has been bringing you down. To begin, ask God to forgive your sin, which is working inside you to poison everything you do. Thank God that his forgiveness is not based on the magnitude of your sin but on the magnitude of his love. No sin is too great for God's complete and unconditional love. Actually, the Bible does mention one unforgivable sin—an attitude of defiant, hostile rejection of God, which prevents you from accepting his forgiveness. Those who don't want his forgiveness are out of its reach. But a heart that truly wants to change is a heart that is ready for the renewal that only God's Spirit can bring.

DIVINE PROMISE

ANYONE WHO BELONGS TO CHRIST HAS
BECOME A NEW PERSON. THE OLD LIFE IS GONE;
A NEW LIFE HAS BEGUN! *2 Corinthians 5:17*

Repentance

MY QUESTION *for* GOD

What is the power of repentance?

A MOMENT *with* GOD

When I refused to confess my sin, my body wasted away, and I groaned all day long. Day and night your hand of discipline was heavy on me. My strength evaporated like water in the summer heat. Finally, I confessed all my sins to you and stopped trying to hide my guilt. I said to myself, "I will confess my rebellion to the LORD." And you forgave me! All my guilt is gone.   PSALM 32:3-5

Zacchaeus stood before the Lord and said, "I will give half my wealth to the poor, Lord, and if I have cheated people on their taxes, I will give them back four times as much!"   LUKE 19:8

God had mercy on me so that Christ Jesus could use me as a prime example of his great patience with even the worst sinners. Then others will realize that they, too, can believe in him and receive eternal life.

1 TIMOTHY 1:16

Repentance means being sorry for sin and being committed to a new way of life—that of serving God. It means turning from a life that is ruled by your selfish thoughts and desires and instead, letting it be ruled by selflessness—possible only by receiving a new nature, which comes when God's Spirit begins to live in you. Repentance is motivated by the realization that you have taken the wrong way in life. The Bible calls this wrong way "sin." Repentance is made complete when you admit your sin and make a commitment, with God's help, to change your life's direction. One of the first essential steps to repentance is confession, which means being humbly honest with God and being sincerely sorry for your sins—the ones you know about and the ones you are unaware of. Confession restores your relationship with God, and this renews your strength and spirit. When you repent, God removes your guilt, restores your joy, and heals your broken soul. A heart that truly longs for change is necessary for repentance to be genuine. When God forgives your sins, you begin your life journey in a new direction without looking back.

DIVINE PROMISE

THERE IS JOY IN THE PRESENCE OF GOD'S
ANGELS WHEN EVEN ONE SINNER REPENTS.
Luke 15:10

Reputation

MY QUESTION *for* GOD

Why should I care what people think of me?

A MOMENT *with* GOD

We are traveling together to guard against any criticism for the way we are handling this generous gift. We are careful to be honorable before the Lord, but we also want everyone else to see that we are honorable.   2 CORINTHIANS 8:20-21

Supplement your faith with a generous provision of moral excellence.   2 PETER 1:5

Work willingly at whatever you do, as though you were working for the Lord rather than for people. Remember that the Lord will give you an inheritance as your reward, and that the Master you are serving is Christ.   COLOSSIANS 3:23-24

*B*elieve it or not, your reputation can actually help you and others experience God. First, any reputation you strive to achieve should result from being fully committed to building spiritual character, not an external change in your life. A reputation built on image without substance eventually becomes a crumbling facade. The key to spiritual strength is to build your life to mirror the character of God. Second, integrity produces credibility. Your testimony of faith means nothing if you have godless character. In fact, others will think you foolish. It is sad how often the message of God is discredited or mocked because of a person's damaged reputation. A godly reputation, built through integrity and humility, spreads the life-changing message of God and the relevancy of his truth. Your life should be the proof others need to be consumed by God's love. Finally, God cares about your reputation. Having a good and honest reputation has many benefits in this life, but it also brings rewards in eternity. It is important to work hard, not to please others but to please God. By doing this, you also honor his reputation. What matters most is not what others think of you but what God thinks of you.

DIVINE PROMISE

MY CHILD, NEVER FORGET THE THINGS I HAVE TAUGHT YOU. STORE MY COMMANDS IN YOUR HEART. . . . NEVER LET LOYALTY AND KINDNESS LEAVE YOU! TIE THEM AROUND YOUR NECK AS A REMINDER. WRITE THEM DEEP WITHIN YOUR HEART. THEN YOU WILL FIND FAVOR WITH BOTH GOD AND PEOPLE, AND YOU WILL EARN A GOOD REPUTATION.   *Proverbs 3:1-4*

Rest

MY QUESTION *for* GOD

Why is it important to rest and what should I do when I rest?

A MOMENT *with* GOD

On the seventh day God had finished his work of creation, so he rested from all his work. And God blessed the seventh day and declared it holy, because it was the day when he rested from all his work of creation.   GENESIS 2:2-3

He lets me rest in green meadows; he leads me beside
peaceful streams. He renews my strength. He guides
me along right paths, bringing honor to his name.

PSALM 23:2-3

Jesus said, "Come to me, all of you who are weary
and carry heavy burdens, and I will give you rest.
Take my yoke upon you. Let me teach you, because I
am humble and gentle at heart, and you will find rest
for your souls. For my yoke is easy to bear, and the
burden I give you is light."   MATTHEW 11:28-30

*R*est is the satisfaction that comes from savoring an
accomplishment—like a gardener after all his fields
are planted, or a builder walking through a completed
home, or an author holding the first printed copy of his
book! In worship we rest as we savor the joy of God's
work and the privilege of working with him. Work is
good, but it must be balanced by regular attention to
worship and the health of our souls. Do you observe
regular times for worship and spiritual refreshment?
God commands that we take time to rest and worship—not because he needs our worship but because
we need the refreshment that worship and rest provide.
God explained this concept in the Ten Commandments
(see Exodus 20:8-10). Good stewardship is careful
management of the resources God has given us, and
rest is one of the resources. Rest is the time to stop
your normal routine to more fully enjoy the renewal
of body, mind, and spirit that comes from time spent
with God and his people.

DIVINE PROMISE

THERE IS A SPECIAL REST STILL WAITING FOR
THE PEOPLE OF GOD. FOR ALL WHO HAVE
ENTERED INTO GOD'S REST HAVE RESTED
FROM THEIR LABORS, JUST AS GOD DID AFTER
CREATING THE WORLD.   *Hebrews 4:9-10*

Risks

MY QUESTION *for* GOD

How do I decide when to live it up and when to play it safe?

A MOMENT *with* GOD

Be careful then, dear brothers and sisters. Make sure
that your own hearts are not evil and unbelieving,
turning you away from the living God.   HEBREWS 3:12

Listen, O Israel! The LORD is our God, the LORD
alone. And you must love the LORD your God with
all your heart, all your soul, and all your strength.

DEUTERONOMY 6:4-5

Faith is the confidence that what we hope for will
actually happen; it gives us assurance about things we
cannot see. Through their faith, the people in days of
old earned a good reputation. . . . It was by faith that
Noah built a large boat to save his family from the
flood. . . . It was by faith that Abraham obeyed when
God called him to leave home and go to another land
that God would give him as his inheritance. . . . It
was by faith that even Sarah was able to have a child,

though she was barren and was too old. She believed
that God would keep his promise.

HEBREWS 11:1-2, 7-8, 11

"*Be* careful crossing the street!" "Be careful driving!"
"Be careful, it's hot!" When you were a child, your
parents may have warned you about the risks of such
behaviors. God, your heavenly father, also warns you
to be careful about your behaviors. His instructions
might be more along the lines of "Be careful not to let
your anger control you" or "Use caution around ungodly people" or "Watch out! Don't let your thoughts
lead you into sin." God gives you clear warnings in the
Bible to guide you away from risky behaviors that could
be hurtful and destructive. But God also encourages
you toward taking certain risks that result in a healthy
and godly life. In these kinds of behaviors, God's Word
tells you to go ahead and take a chance. God might say,
"Go ahead. Attend that college that keeps popping into
your mind. Take that mission trip, accept that job, help
that person, accept that challenge." Taking that risk is
taking a step of faith to perhaps do the very thing God
wants you to do. Taking the risks that help you grow in
your faith and avoiding risks that you know will harm
your walk with God will turn your life into a healthy
and rich adventure. What a divine moment it is to take
a risk and find God in it.

DIVINE PROMISE

COMMIT EVERYTHING YOU DO TO THE LORD.
TRUST HIM, AND HE WILL HELP YOU.   *Psalm 37:5*

Romance

MY QUESTION *for* GOD

Where's the romance in a life of faith?

A MOMENT *with* GOD

Long ago the LORD said to Israel: "I have loved you,
my people, with an everlasting love. With unfailing
love I have drawn you to myself."   JEREMIAH 31:3

I will win her back once again. I will lead her into
the desert and speak tenderly to her there. . . . I will
make you my wife forever, showing you righteousness
and justice, unfailing love and compassion. I will
be faithful to you and make you mine, and you will
finally know me as the LORD.   HOSEA 2:14, 19-20

The LORD said to me, "Go and love your wife again,
even though she commits adultery with another lover.
This will illustrate that the LORD still loves Israel,
even though the people have turned to other gods and
love to worship them."   HOSEA 3:1

For husbands, this means love your wives, just as
Christ loved the church.   EPHESIANS 5:25

Let us be glad and rejoice, and let us give honor to him. For the time has come for the wedding feast of the Lamb, and his bride has prepared herself.

REVELATION 19:7

We know how much God loves us, and we have put our trust in his love. God is love, and all who live in love live in God, and God lives in them.   1 JOHN 4:16

*R*omance is the language of love that fosters intimacy with another person. What a wonderful feeling it is when someone expresses affection for you, enjoys your company, and is captivated by you. You feel confident, strong, and interesting to that person. As you read through the Bible, you learn that God himself is a romantic who desires an intimate relationship with you. He desires your constant company and is interested in the smallest details of your life. He wants nothing more than to walk with you through this life and for eternity. As you realize your preciousness to God, you will find confidence in your faith, strength to be faithful to him, and a deep hunger and desire to know more of him.

DIVINE PROMISE

SURELY YOUR GOODNESS AND UNFAILING LOVE WILL PURSUE ME ALL THE DAYS OF MY LIFE, AND I WILL LIVE IN THE HOUSE OF THE LORD FOREVER. *Psalm 23:6*

Sacred

MY QUESTIONS *for* GOD

When is something sacred? What does it mean to be sacred?

A MOMENT *with* GOD

Finally, they made the sacred medallion—the badge of holiness—of pure gold. They engraved it like a seal with these words: HOLY TO THE LORD.

EXODUS 39:30

Do not make idols or set up carved images, or sacred pillars, or sculptured stones in your land so you may worship them. I am the LORD your God. LEVITICUS 26:1

Don't you realize that your body is the temple of the Holy Spirit, who lives in you and was given to you by God? 1 CORINTHIANS 6:19

Sacred means set apart for God or dedicated for the purposes of God. When objects are deemed sacred, it usually means they are regarded with respect and honor. In Exodus 39:30, the sacred medallion served as a visual reminder to the Israelites that they were to be set apart as God's special nation. However, sacred objects can also become "defiled" when they become mere religious rituals rather than spiritual reminders. The Israelites soon began making other "sacred" objects and worshiped these objects rather than the God the objects pointed to (see Judges 2:11-12). You are set apart for God. Your body is the dwelling place of God's

Holy Spirit, and it can become either sacred or defiled.
When you keep yourself pure and dedicate yourself to
God, each day your life becomes more sacred as you
commit yourself to God's purposes.

DIVINE PROMISE

MAY THE GOD OF PEACE MAKE YOU HOLY IN
EVERY WAY, AND MAY YOUR WHOLE SPIRIT
AND SOUL AND BODY BE KEPT BLAMELESS
UNTIL OUR LORD JESUS CHRIST COMES AGAIN.
1 Thessalonians 5:23

Sacrifice

MY QUESTION *for* GOD

Are there things I should sacrifice in order to serve God?

A MOMENT *with* GOD

The world would love you as one of its own if you
belonged to it, but you are no longer part of the
world. I chose you to come out of the world, so it
hates you. Do you remember what I told you? 'A slave
is not greater than the master.' Since they persecuted
me, naturally they will persecute you. And if they
had listened to me, they would listen to you. They
will do all this to you because of me, for they have
rejected the One who sent me.   JOHN 15:19-21

As for me, my life has already been poured out as an offering to God.

2 TIMOTHY 4:6

Don't forget to do good and to share with those in need. These are the sacrifices that please God.

HEBREWS 13:16

Since those who don't know God can't understand his ways, you may find that you have to sacrifice popularity in order to obey God. God doesn't want your friendship only when it's convenient for you. He requires your complete devotion to him, and that may mean sacrificing aspects of your relationships with those who do not understand God. When you find yourself in this situation, remember what God gave up for you—his Son. It is often through giving up something for someone else that you can come to better understand the great sacrifice God has made for you.

DIVINE PROMISE

EVERYONE WHO HAS GIVEN UP HOUSES OR BROTHERS OR SISTERS OR FATHER OR MOTHER OR CHILDREN OR PROPERTY, FOR MY SAKE, WILL RECEIVE A HUNDRED TIMES AS MUCH IN RETURN AND WILL INHERIT ETERNAL LIFE.

Matthew 19:29

Salvation

How should my salvation affect my daily life?

A MOMENT *with* GOD

We know that our old sinful selves were crucified
with Christ so that sin might lose its power in our
lives. We are no longer slaves to sin. For when we
died with Christ we were set free from the power of
sin. And since we died with Christ, we know we will
also live with him. We are sure of this because Christ
was raised from the dead, and he will never die again.
Death no longer has any power over him. When he
died, he died once to break the power of sin. But
now that he lives, he lives for the glory of God.

ROMANS 6:6-10

He has created us anew in Christ Jesus, so we can do
the good things he planned for us long ago.

EPHESIANS 2:10

Since we have been made right in God's sight by faith,
we have peace with God because of what Jesus Christ
our Lord has done for us.   ROMANS 5:1

If someone told you that you had to work until retirement age but when you reached that age, you would
inherit several million dollars, it would change the way
you live now. You would worry less, be more confident, maybe take greater risks, be more generous, have

greater peace of mind. It would probably also affect the kind of job you chose. When you are saved, by accepting Jesus Christ as Lord, you have just guaranteed an inheritance of eternal life in a perfect world, with everything you could want or need. This inheritance should change the way you live. You are now able to discover and take part in the plan that God has for you, a plan he worked out especially for you since the beginning of time. You can worry less and be more confident that nothing can truly harm your soul or your eternal future. You can take some risks when you think God is asking you to do something for him. You can be more generous and experience more peace of mind. Too often, those who have experienced salvation live as if they haven't. Live as if your future is all you could ever want, for that is exactly the case.

DIVINE PROMISE

ANYONE WHO BELONGS TO CHRIST HAS BECOME A NEW PERSON. THE OLD LIFE IS GONE; A NEW LIFE HAS BEGUN! *2 Corinthians 5:17*

Satisfaction

MY QUESTION *for* GOD

Why can't I ever feel satisfied with my life?

A MOMENT *with* GOD

Everything is wearisome beyond description. No
matter how much we see, we are never satisfied.
No matter how much we hear, we are not content.

ECCLESIASTES 1:8

Why spend your money on food that does not give
you strength? Why pay for food that does you no
good? Listen to me, and you will eat what is good.
You will enjoy the finest food. Come to me with your
ears wide open. Listen, and you will find life.

ISAIAH 55:2-3

You don't have what you want because you don't ask
God for it. And even when you ask, you don't get it
because your motives are all wrong—you want only
what will give you pleasure.   JAMES 4:2-3

The Holy Spirit produces this kind of fruit in our
lives: love, joy, peace, patience, kindness, goodness,
faithfulness, gentleness, and self-control.

GALATIANS 5:22-23

The voice said to me, "Son of man, eat what I am
giving you—eat this scroll! Then go and give its
message to the people of Israel." So I opened my
mouth, and he fed me the scroll. "Fill your stomach
with this," he said. And when I ate it, it tasted as
sweet as honey in my mouth. . . . Then he added,
"Son of man, let all my words sink deep into your
own heart first. Listen to them carefully for yourself."

EZEKIEL 3:1-3, 10

*T*oo many people try to meet their deepest needs in ways that just don't satisfy. The Bible often uses the metaphor of food to explain what happens when you try to satisfy your desires in the wrong way. When you are hungry, your body is craving good food, and eating only candy will never truly satisfy your cravings. You may get shaky, your body won't function well, and if you never eat anything healthy, you'll suffer long-term physical damage. The same principle applies to satisfying your hungry soul. Fill it only with fun, pleasure, and sin, and you'll always be craving something more. Your soul will be weak and shaky, and it won't function well. You need a steady diet of "soul" food—eating up God's Word, quenching your thirst with him so his Holy Spirit can fill you with the things that will make you a strong, mature man or woman of faith. Only God's way of life will truly satisfy your deepest longings because God created you to be in relationship with him. When you have satisfied your soul with God, you will have the strength and wisdom to take advantage of the opportunities he sends your way to truly make a difference. And you can be sure that the satisfaction you feel will be sustained since it comes directly from God.

DIVINE PROMISE

HE SATISFIES THE THIRSTY AND FILLS THE HUNGRY WITH GOOD THINGS. *Psalm 107:9*

Self-Control

MY QUESTION *for* GOD

I'm not a disciplined person; how can I possibly learn self-control?

A MOMENT *with* GOD

We must live decent lives for all to see. Don't participate in the darkness of wild parties and drunkenness, or in sexual promiscuity and immoral living, or in quarreling and jealousy. Instead, clothe yourself with the presence of the Lord Jesus Christ. And don't let yourself think about ways to indulge your evil desires.   ROMANS 13:13-14

Athletes cannot win the prize unless they follow the rules.   2 TIMOTHY 2:5

All athletes are disciplined in their training. They do it to win a prize that will fade away, but we do it for an eternal prize.   1 CORINTHIANS 9:25

Self-control first involves knowing God's guidelines for right living as found in the Bible. You need to know what it is you must control before you can keep it un-der control. God wants you to exercise self-control over what you think, what you say, and what you do. He wants you to live as his child, not as someone who mindlessly follows whatever fad the culture is currently glorifying. You can do this by (1) honestly assessing your weaknesses, (2) determining that they will no longer rule you, (3) appealing to the Holy Spirit to help you stand strong against temptation, (4) removing yourself from places of temptation, (5) humbly confessing to God when you make a mistake, and (6) giving glory to God when you are victorious!

DIVINE PROMISE

SUPPLEMENT YOUR FAITH WITH A GENEROUS PROVISION OF MORAL EXCELLENCE, AND MORAL EXCELLENCE WITH KNOWLEDGE, AND KNOWLEDGE WITH SELF-CONTROL, AND SELF-CONTROL WITH PATIENT ENDURANCE, AND PATIENT ENDURANCE WITH GODLINESS, AND GODLINESS WITH BROTHERLY AFFECTION, AND BROTHERLY AFFECTION WITH LOVE FOR EVERYONE. THE MORE YOU GROW LIKE THIS, THE MORE PRODUCTIVE AND USEFUL YOU WILL BE IN YOUR KNOWLEDGE OF OUR LORD JESUS CHRIST. *2 Peter 1:5-8*

Serving Others

MY QUESTION *for* GOD

What really happens when I serve others?

A MOMENT *with* GOD

I am the true grapevine, and my Father is the gardener. . . . Remain in me, and I will remain in you. For a branch cannot produce fruit if it is severed from the vine, and you cannot be fruitful unless

you remain in me. Yes, I am the vine; you are the
branches. Those who remain in me, and I in them,
will produce much fruit. For apart from me you can
do nothing.   JOHN 15:1, 4-5

You have been called to live in freedom, my brothers
and sisters. But don't use your freedom to satisfy your
sinful nature. Instead, use your freedom to serve one
another in love.   GALATIANS 5:13

Among you it will be different. Whoever wants to
be a leader among you must be your servant. . . . For
even the Son of Man came not to be served but to
serve others and to give his life as a ransom for many.

MATTHEW 20:26-28

A popular notion of success is being able to afford
the luxury of having servants. Jesus turns this thinking on its head by teaching that the highest goal in life
is to *be* a servant. He places such a high value on serving because instead of being self-centered, it is others-
centered, which is the essence of effective Christian
living. When you are connected to Jesus, he turns your
simple acts into something profound and purposeful.
He turns your simple act of singing into a profound
chorus of praise that ministers to an entire congregation. He turns your simple act of placing your tithe in
the offering plate into a profound act of mercy that will
touch the heart of the needy person who receives it. He
turns your simple act of teaching children in Sunday
school into a profound moment in the heart of a child

who suddenly realizes the need for salvation. He turns your simple act of visiting shut-ins into a divine moment of encouragement. When you step out to serve, God turns your simple acts of service into profound works for his Kingdom.

DIVINE PROMISE

ALL GLORY TO GOD, WHO IS ABLE, THROUGH HIS MIGHTY POWER AT WORK WITHIN US, TO ACCOMPLISH INFINITELY MORE THAN WE MIGHT ASK OR THINK. *Ephesians 3:20*

Sharing

MY QUESTION *for* GOD

How can I share with others when I don't have much to give?

A MOMENT *with* GOD

He makes the whole body fit together perfectly. As each part does its own special work, it helps the other parts grow, so that the whole body is healthy and growing and full of love. EPHESIANS 4:16

On the first day of each week, you should each put aside a portion of the money you have earned.

1 CORINTHIANS 16:2

You must each decide in your heart how much to give. And don't give reluctantly or in response to pressure. "For God loves a person who gives cheerfully."   2 CORINTHIANS 9:7

𝓔ven if you don't have much materially, you still have resources available to you: your time, your talents, your thoughts, your friendship, your testimony, your faith, your encouraging words. Even if you feel that what you have to offer is small in comparison with what others may have, have faith that God can multiply your gifts as you combine your efforts alongside other members of the church body. When it does come to making financial contributions, trying to quantify how much you should give reflects the wrong attitude. God's desire is that you will want to give to others generously. Those who do so discover that the benefits of giving are far greater than the temporary satisfaction of receiving.

DIVINE PROMISE

IF YOU GIVE EVEN A CUP OF COLD WATER TO
ONE OF THE LEAST OF MY FOLLOWERS, YOU
WILL SURELY BE REWARDED.   *Matthew 10:42*

𝓢ilence

MY QUESTION *for* GOD

Sometimes I feel as if God is being silent. Why doesn't he respond?

A Moment *with* God

Listen! The Lord's arm is not too weak to save you,
nor is his ear too deaf to hear you call. It's your sins
that have cut you off from God. Because of your sins,
he has turned away and will not listen anymore.

Isaiah 59:1-2

The Lord isn't really being slow about his promise, as
some people think. No, he is being patient for your
sake. He does not want anyone to be destroyed, but
wants everyone to repent.   2 Peter 3:9

Wait patiently for the Lord. Be brave and
courageous. Yes, wait patiently for the Lord.

Psalm 27:14

When God seems silent, it may mean that he is patiently waiting for you to act—to turn away from a
sinful habit, to follow a call that he has made perfectly
clear, or to just stop to listen to him. If you are persist-
ing in a sinful habit, you will continue to move further
away from God, which will make it much harder to
hear him. If God isn't answering you, it may be time
to change direction and move toward him, not away.
Sometimes, however, you make an honest request, and
God doesn't seem to answer. It can be easy to interpret
God's answers of "no" or "wait" as silence. But the fact
that you make an honest request doesn't necessarily
mean that what you are asking is good for you. Finally,
God could be silent because he wants you to take a

step of faith and trust him. You may have several good options, and God will be pleased to go with you whichever option you choose. Sometimes he doesn't want to make his answer clear because that would be too easy, and your faith in him won't grow. Although you may never understand why God seems silent at times, don't give up and leave him, because he hasn't left you. Use the opportunity to draw closer to him, and continue to listen carefully for what he wants you to learn.

DIVINE PROMISE

AS FOR ME, I LOOK TO THE LORD FOR HELP.
I WAIT CONFIDENTLY FOR GOD TO SAVE ME,
AND MY GOD WILL CERTAINLY HEAR ME.
Micah 7:7

Sin

MY QUESTIONS *for* GOD

What is sin? What is so bad about it?

A MOMENT *with* GOD

The wages of sin is death, but the free gift of God is eternal life through Christ Jesus our Lord. ROMANS 6:23

He was pierced for our rebellion, crushed for our sins. He was beaten so we could be whole. He was whipped so we could be healed. All of us, like sheep, have strayed away. We have left God's paths to

follow our own. Yet the LORD laid on him the sins of
us all.   ISAIAH 53:5-6

Temptation comes from our own desires, which
entice us and drag us away. These desires give birth
to sinful actions. And when sin is allowed to grow, it
gives birth to death.   JAMES 1:14-15

Sin is both serious and dangerous. Simply put, sin
is rebellion against God. It not only ruins your life on
earth; it is also the cause of spiritual death. But what
does it mean to sin? You can spend a lot of time debat-
ing what sin is, but you may find it more helpful to
focus on your relationship with God. When you do,
sin will become obvious because it is those thoughts
and actions that disobey and disappoint him. In the
same way that ignoring or hurting a close friend will
harm the relationship, ignoring and disappointing God
by choosing your own way in life instead of his way
will harm your relationship with him. If you engage in
thoughts and actions that lead to time with God and
deepen your relationship with him, you are probably
on the right track. But if your thoughts and actions
are violating God's rules for life as found in the Bible
and are thus harming your relationship with God, then
you are engaging in some form of sin. The good news
is that if you confess your sins to God and ask for forgiveness, he will immediately restore your relationship
with him. Everyone sins, so asking for forgiveness is
something you should do on a regular basis, along with
praying that God will help you to engage in thoughts

and actions that will please and obey him and thus strengthen your relationship with him.

DIVINE PROMISE

IF WE CONFESS OUR SINS TO HIM, HE IS FAITHFUL AND JUST TO FORGIVE US OUR SINS AND TO CLEANSE US FROM ALL WICKEDNESS. *1 John 1:9*

Spiritual Blindness

MY QUESTIONS *for* GOD

What causes spiritual blindness? How can I see with spiritual eyes?

A MOMENT *with* GOD

Sin whispers to the wicked, deep within their hearts. They have no fear of God at all. In their blind conceit, they cannot see how wicked they really are. PSALM 36:1-2

I let them follow their own stubborn desires, living according to their own ideas.   PSALM 81:12

Satan, who is the god of this world, has blinded the minds of those who don't believe. They are unable to see the glorious light of the Good News. They don't understand this message about the glory of Christ, who is the exact likeness of God.   2 CORINTHIANS 4:4

Jesus told him, "I entered this world to render
judgment—to give sight to the blind and to show
those who think they see that they are blind."

JOHN 9:39

*W*hen you get in the habit of sinning and it doesn't
bother you and you lose your fear of God, you won't
be aware of a terrible change going on in your heart.
This way of living leads to pride, which leads to self-
centeredness, which will narrow your field of spiritual
vision and eventually blind you completely to what's
really important. Satan knows how to cause spiritual
blindness in those who don't believe in God. He closes
their ears to hearing and understanding God and his
plan for the world, and he causes them to be unim-
pressed by God's people and unaware of God's work
all around them. As a result, unbelief blinds them to
God's existence and involvement in the world and in
their lives. They will stumble through life with no understanding of where they are ultimately going because
they don't have truth as their compass. They are blind
to the real purpose of life. On the other hand, spiritual
vision is connected to a humble heart. When you recognize that your own way is not best and that you need
divine help, God opens your spiritual eyes to his ways,
lights the proper path ahead of you, and guides you as
you trust his directions for your life.

DIVINE PROMISE

YOU WILL SHOW ME THE WAY OF LIFE,
GRANTING ME THE JOY OF YOUR PRESENCE
AND THE PLEASURES OF LIVING WITH
YOU FOREVER.   *Psalm 16:11*

Spiritual Gifts

MY QUESTIONS *for* GOD

What are my spiritual gifts? What happens when I use them?

A MOMENT *with* GOD

The LORD has filled Bezalel with the Spirit of God,
giving him great wisdom, ability, and expertise in all
kinds of crafts. He is a master craftsman, expert in
working with gold, silver, and bronze.   EXODUS 35:31-32

In his grace, God has given us different gifts for
doing certain things well. So if God has given you
the ability to prophesy, speak out with as much faith
as God has given you. If your gift is serving others,
serve them well. If you are a teacher, teach well. If
your gift is to encourage others, be encouraging. If
it is giving, give generously. If God has given you
leadership ability, take the responsibility seriously.
And if you have a gift for showing kindness to others,
do it gladly.   ROMANS 12:6-8

Make the most of every opportunity in these evil
days. Don't act thoughtlessly, but understand what
the Lord wants you to do.   EPHESIANS 5:16-17

*B*eing available to God includes the continual development of the gifts he has given you so that you will be prepared for him to use you. It involves your willingness to use those gifts to serve him in the calling he currently has for you. Do you know the unique gifts God has given you? If not, take a spiritual-gifts assessment and ask your friends what they think your spiritual gifts are. It is important to know that God gives each individual a spiritual gift (sometimes more than one!) and a special ministry in the church where you can use those gifts to help and encourage others and to bring glory to his name. These specific spiritual gifts help you fulfill the purpose for which God made you. You never use these spiritual gifts up; rather, the more you use them, the more they grow and allow you to make a unique contribution in your sphere of influence. Using your spiritual gifts is a divine moment where you find the "sweet spot" of your effectiveness for God and you do your best work for him when you help others.

Divine Promise

GOD HAS GIVEN EACH OF YOU A GIFT FROM HIS GREAT VARIETY OF SPIRITUAL GIFTS. USE THEM WELL TO SERVE ONE ANOTHER. DO YOU HAVE THE GIFT OF SPEAKING? THEN SPEAK AS THOUGH GOD HIMSELF WERE SPEAKING THROUGH YOU. DO YOU HAVE THE GIFT OF HELPING OTHERS? DO IT WITH ALL THE STRENGTH AND ENERGY THAT GOD SUPPLIES. THEN EVERYTHING YOU DO WILL BRING GLORY TO GOD THROUGH JESUS CHRIST.   *1 Peter 4:10-11*

Spiritual Warfare

MY QUESTION for GOD

In spiritual warfare, how do I fight back?

A MOMENT with GOD

Jesus told him, "No! The Scriptures say. . . ." Jesus responded, "The Scriptures also say, 'You must not test the LORD your God.'" . . . "Get out of here, Satan," Jesus told him. "For the Scriptures say . . ."

MATTHEW 4: 4, 7, 10

Put on salvation as your helmet, and take the sword of the Spirit, which is the word of God.   EPHESIANS 6:17

Be strong in the Lord and in his mighty power. Put on all of God's armor so that you will be able to stand firm against all strategies of the devil. For we are not fighting against flesh-and-blood enemies, but against evil rulers and authorities of the unseen world, against mighty powers in this dark world, and against evil spirits in the heavenly places.   EPHESIANS 6:10-12

Your best offensive weapon is the Word of God. It's odd to think of the Bible as a weapon, but in it God reveals his plan of attack against evil. It's your battle plan; if you don't read it, you won't know how to fight the battle that can determine your destiny, here on earth and for eternity. The Bible exposes the enemy, Satan, for who he is, shines the light of God's truth on his lies, teaches you how to prepare for his attacks, and makes you wise against his tricks and strategies. Only by knowing who you are fighting, where the battle is, and how to defend yourself will you be able to win. It is vital to read God's Word as regularly as possible. This weapon will send Satan running for cover.

DIVINE PROMISE

THE LORD IS FAITHFUL; HE WILL STRENGTHEN YOU AND GUARD YOU FROM THE EVIL ONE.

2 Thessalonians 3:3

Suffering

MY QUESTION *for* GOD

Can any good come from suffering?

A MOMENT *with* GOD

We can rejoice, too, when we run into problems and trials, for we know that they help us develop endurance. And endurance develops strength of character, and character strengthens our confident hope of salvation.   ROMANS 5:3-4

We don't look at the troubles we can see now; rather, we fix our gaze on things that cannot be seen. For the things we see now will soon be gone, but the things we cannot see will last forever.   2 CORINTHIANS 4:18

All praise to God, the Father of our Lord Jesus Christ. God is our merciful Father and the source of all comfort. He comforts us in all our troubles.

2 CORINTHIANS 1:3-4

*I*t makes sense that a pleasure-seeking society would try to avoid suffering at any cost. But it is through suffering, like other challenges, that you grow. No one likes pain and adversity because they challenge you physically, mentally, emotionally, and spiritually. But those who have gone through such taxing times are stronger and wiser for those experiences. An athlete or a musician will never achieve greatness without painful hours of practice. Likewise, you will never become strong and wise without being pushed, shoved, and hurt by life's troubles. While God never wants to see you suffer, he sometimes allows painful and adverse times in your life in order to strengthen your character and faith. God uses suffering to expand your perspective and turn your thoughts heavenward, to strengthen your faith as you hope expectantly for his promises to come true. Often it is not until you reach the other side of suffering that you can appreciate the perspective and growth that have come as a result of suffering.

DIVINE PROMISE

IN HIS KINDNESS GOD CALLED YOU TO SHARE IN HIS ETERNAL GLORY BY MEANS OF CHRIST JESUS. SO AFTER YOU HAVE SUFFERED A LITTLE WHILE, HE WILL RESTORE, SUPPORT, AND

STRENGTHEN YOU, AND HE WILL PLACE YOU
ON A FIRM FOUNDATION.   *1 Peter 5:10*

Supernatural

MY QUESTION *for* GOD

Can I ever experience the supernatural?

A MOMENT *with* GOD

Whenever someone turns to the Lord, the veil is
taken away. For the Lord is the Spirit, and wherever
the Spirit of the Lord is, there is freedom. So all of
us who have had that veil removed can see and reflect
the glory of the Lord. And the Lord—who is the
Spirit—makes us more and more like him as we are
changed into his glorious image.   2 CORINTHIANS 3:16-18

When you believed in Christ, he identified you as
his own by giving you the Holy Spirit, whom he
promised long ago. The Spirit is God's guarantee that
he will give us the inheritance he promised and that
he has purchased us to be his own people. He did this
so we would praise and glorify him.   EPHESIANS 1:13-14

The Holy Spirit produces this kind of fruit in our
lives: love, joy, peace, patience, kindness, goodness,
faithfulness, gentleness, and self-control.

GALATIANS 5:22-23

God's presence within you, in the form of the Holy Spirit, is evidence of the supernatural. The Holy Spirit teaches and instructs your heart in the ways of God and reveals things to you that you cannot see with your physical eyes. The Holy Spirit gives you the power to recognize how God works and empowers you in life-changing ways: to love others even when they wrong you, to find overwhelming peace in the midst of great suffering, to think of others before yourself. The Holy Spirit gives you the assurance that there is a God, that he is at work in the world, and that you belong to him if you believe.

DIVINE PROMISE

WE HAVE RECEIVED GOD'S SPIRIT (NOT THE WORLD'S SPIRIT), SO WE CAN KNOW THE WONDERFUL THINGS GOD HAS FREELY GIVEN US.   *1 Corinthians 2:12*

Surrender

MY QUESTIONS *for* GOD

What is the paradox of surrender? Why must I give something up?

A MOMENT *with* GOD

If you try to hang on to your life, you will lose it. But if you give up your life for my sake, you will save it.

MATTHEW 16:25

Peter said, "We've left our homes to follow you." "Yes," Jesus replied, "and I assure you that everyone who has given up house or wife or brothers or parents or children, for the sake of the Kingdom of God, will be repaid many times over in this life, and will have eternal life in the world to come."   LUKE 18:28-30

What do you benefit if you gain the whole world but are yourself lost or destroyed?   LUKE 9:25

When you surrender your life, your heart, and your desires to God, you are not left empty. Surrendering your life doesn't mean not having a life. In fact, God gives you a new life far better than your old one. He fills your heart with joy and replaces your old desires with new and more beautiful ones. Surrendering to God stretches life so you can have more of it, and it fills you to overflowing with joy. You receive a new and better life by giving up your old one. When you surrender your temporary life here on earth to God, he gives you eternal life in exchange.

DIVINE PROMISE

IT IS NO LONGER I WHO LIVE, BUT CHRIST LIVES IN ME. SO I LIVE IN THIS EARTHLY BODY BY TRUSTING IN THE SON OF GOD, WHO LOVED ME AND GAVE HIMSELF FOR ME.
Galatians 2:20

Temptation

MY QUESTION *for* GOD

Do I have the power to resist temptation?

A MOMENT *with* GOD

The Spirit who lives in you is greater than the spirit
who lives in the world.   1 JOHN 4:4

Every child of God defeats this evil world, and we
achieve this victory through our faith. And who can
win this battle against the world? Only those who
believe that Jesus is the Son of God.   1 JOHN 5:4-5

The temptations in your life are no different from
what others experience. And God is faithful. He will
not allow the temptation to be more than you can
stand. When you are tempted, he will show you a
way out so that you can endure.   1 CORINTHIANS 10:13

Satan has the power to overwhelm you if it's just you
against him. But with Jesus, Satan has no power. When
Jesus lives "in you" in the form of the Holy Spirit, his
power becomes available to you, and then Satan can be
overwhelmed. Now you have the advantage in overcoming any temptation. The devil can tempt you, but
he cannot coerce you. He can dangle the bait in front of
you, but he cannot force you to take it. He'll try every
trick in the book to make you think you're missing
out, that you cannot and should not resist. But you can
break free from temptation when you change your fo-

cus from what's in front of you to who is inside of you. Then you can discern the difference between the lies of temptation and the truth of God's Word, between what seems so right and what's really right. Instead of thinking about what you're missing out on, think about what you'll be gaining by obeying God and resisting temptation. You have far more power available to you than you think. When you arm yourself with God's Word and rely on the presence of his Spirit within you, temptations become divine moments in which you can experience the power of God helping you resist.

DIVINE PROMISE

RESIST THE DEVIL, AND HE WILL FLEE
FROM YOU.   *James 4:7*

Testing

MY QUESTION *for* GOD

How does God test my faith?

A MOMENT *with* GOD

It was by faith that Abraham obeyed when God called him to leave home and go to another land that God would give him as his inheritance. He went without knowing where he was going.   HEBREWS 11:8

When ambassadors arrived from Babylon to ask about the remarkable events that had taken place in the

land, God withdrew from Hezekiah in order to test
him and to see what was really in his heart.

2 CHRONICLES 32:31

I have refined you, but not as silver is refined. Rather,
I have refined you in the furnace of suffering.

ISAIAH 48:10

A car doesn't receive a five-star safety rating unless
it's undergone numerous crash tests and achieved high
scores. With each test, changes and adjustments are
made to ensure that if you ever have an accident, you
have a better chance of surviving. Because of the testing, you are confident that the air bags will open on
impact, that the car is less likely to roll over, and that
the steel beams in the doors will better protect your
body. Quality products undergo many tests to ensure
that they can stand up to everyday stress. It shouldn't
be a surprise to us that this same principle applies to
people. When you are tested—through stress, pressure, suffering, pain—you learn to make adjustments
and changes that make you stronger for real living. God
sometimes tests you in order to help you grow stronger
and more mature in your faith. He tests you in different ways. First, he may test you through incomplete
information about himself or his ways. Just as you don't
need to know everything about electricity to turn on
a light, so you need not know everything about God's
ways to trust his promises to do what is best for you.
The question he asks is, "Can your faith remain strong
even when you don't know all the facts?" Second, God

may test your faith through silence. Sometimes what God *doesn't* say may be more effective in getting your attention than what he *does* say. God's eloquence is the effectiveness of his communication, not the quantity of his words. God's silence may be his way of drawing you closer to him in faith. God may also test you through suffering. The depth of your faith will be revealed by your response to trials and troubling times. Of course, no one wants troubles in life, but most of us desire the strengthening benefits and rewards they bring. How you endure suffering reveals your level of maturity and faith.

DIVINE PROMISE

GOD BLESSES THOSE WHO PATIENTLY ENDURE TESTING AND TEMPTATION. AFTERWARD THEY WILL RECEIVE THE CROWN OF LIFE THAT GOD HAS PROMISED TO THOSE WHO LOVE HIM.

James 1:12

Thankfulness

MY QUESTION *for* GOD

What are the blessings of a thankful attitude?

A MOMENT *with* GOD

Giving thanks is a sacrifice that truly honors me. If you keep to my path, I will reveal to you the salvation of God.

PSALM 50:23

It is good to give thanks to the LORD, to sing praises
to the Most High.   PSALM 92:1

Even though the fig trees have no blossoms, and there
are no grapes on the vines; even though the olive
crop fails, and the fields lie empty and barren; even
though the flocks die in the fields, and the cattle
barns are empty, yet I will rejoice in the LORD! I will
be joyful in the God of my salvation! The Sovereign
LORD is my strength! He makes me as surefooted as a
deer, able to tread upon the heights.   HABAKKUK 3:17-19

The blessing of a spirit of gratitude is a new outlook
on life. Thankfulness changes the way you look at your
circumstances. Complaining connects you to unhappi-
ness—gratitude and praise connect you to the source
of real joy. When you make thanksgiving a regular part
of your life, you stay focused on what God has done
and continues to do for you. Expressing gratitude for
God's help is a form of worship. When you give thanks
to God, you honor and praise him for what he has done
in your life, in the lives of others, in the church, and
in the world. Similarly, you honor others when you
give thanks to them and respect them for who they
are and what they have done. This attitude of gratitude
prevents you from expecting others to serve you and
allows you to enjoy whatever blessings come your way.
An attitude of thankfulness not only brings blessings
to your life, but it also blesses others with appreciation
and honor.

DIVINE CHALLENGE

BE THANKFUL IN ALL CIRCUMSTANCES, FOR
THIS IS GOD'S WILL FOR YOU WHO BELONG
TO CHRIST JESUS.   *1 Thessalonians 5:18*

Thoughts

MY QUESTION *for* GOD

How do my thoughts affect my actions?

A MOMENT *with* GOD

[Jesus] added, "It is what comes from inside that
defiles you. For from within, out of a person's heart,
come evil thoughts, sexual immorality, theft, murder,
adultery, greed, wickedness, deceit, lustful desires,
envy, slander, pride, and foolishness. All these vile
things come from within; they are what defile you."

MARK 7:20-23

Now, dear brothers and sisters, one final thing. Fix
your thoughts on what is true, and honorable, and
right, and pure, and lovely, and admirable. Think
about things that are excellent and worthy of praise.
Keep putting into practice all you learned and
received from me—everything you heard from me
and saw me doing. Then the God of peace will be
with you.

PHILIPPIANS 4:8-9

What you do comes from what you think about. The seeds for your actions, both good and bad, are planted in your heart. As these seeds grow, their nature is revealed by the fruit they produce: the things you say and do. Nurture the soil of your heart and mind to produce thoughts that are pleasing to God. As you think, so you are, and so you become. Your conduct is shaped by your character, and your character is shaped by the condition of your heart. As God transforms you from the inside out, your actions will be transformed as well.

DIVINE PROMISE

YOU WILL KEEP IN PERFECT PEACE ALL WHO TRUST IN YOU, ALL WHOSE THOUGHTS ARE FIXED ON YOU!   *Isaiah 26:3*

Time

MY QUESTION *for* GOD

How can I make the most meaningful use of the time I have?

A MOMENT *with* GOD

LORD, remind me how brief my time on earth will be. Remind me that my days are numbered—how fleeting my life is. You have made my life no longer than the width of my hand. My entire lifetime is just a moment to you; at best, each of us is but a breath. . . . And so, Lord, where do I put my hope? My only hope is in you.   PSALM 39:4-7

Be careful how you live. Don't live like fools,
but like those who are wise. Make the most of
every opportunity in these evil days. Don't act
thoughtlessly, but understand what the Lord wants
you to do. Don't be drunk with wine, because that
will ruin your life. Instead, be filled with the Holy
Spirit, singing psalms and hymns and spiritual songs
among yourselves, and making music to the Lord in
your hearts.   EPHESIANS 5:15-19

Those who are wise will find a time and a way to
do what is right, for there is a time and a way for
everything, even when a person is in trouble.

ECCLESIASTES 8:5-6

*T*ime is a lot like battery energy—you rarely know
how much is left until it's gone. With time, unlike
batteries, you cannot buy more or borrow some from
someone else. That is why time is so valuable, and yet
most of us live as if it means very little. You probably
feel you waste far too much time doing what does not
seem most important or significant, and you know you
should be more purposeful about how you spend it.
Maybe you're unsure how to live more purposefully.
The Bible is clear that how you use your precious time
on earth will have an impact on your life in heaven.
You may live by the motto "So much to do, so little
time." But God does not ask you to do everything, just
everything he has called you to do, and he assures you
that there is time for whatever it is. The more you invest in discovering the purpose for which God created

you and how to live out that purpose with obedience and responsibility, the more meaningful and significant your time on earth will become.

DIVINE PROMISE

TEACH US TO REALIZE THE BREVITY OF LIFE, SO THAT WE MAY GROW IN WISDOM.   *Psalm 90:12*

Tired

MY QUESTION *for* GOD

How can I find peaceful rest?

A MOMENT *with* GOD

He gives power to the weak and strength to the powerless. Even youths will become weak and tired, and young men will fall in exhaustion. But those who trust in the LORD will find new strength. They will soar high on wings like eagles. They will run and not grow weary. They will walk and not faint.

ISAIAH 40:29-31

I have given rest to the weary and joy to the sorrowing.   JEREMIAH 31:25

Jesus said, "Come to me, all of you who are weary and carry heavy burdens, and I will give you rest."

MATTHEW 11:28

I replied, "But my work seems so useless! I have spent my strength for nothing and to no purpose. Yet I leave it all in the LORD's hand; I will trust God for my reward."

ISAIAH 49:4

*G*od will give you renewed strength when you grow weary. When you come to him in praise, he refreshes your heart. When you come to him in prayer, he refreshes your soul. When you come to him in meditation, he refreshes your mind. When you come to him in solitude, he refreshes your body. When you come to him with thankfulness, he refreshes your perspective. Practicing these disciplines releases the burdens of life and draws strength from God, the source of strength.

DIVINE PROMISE

I LAY DOWN AND SLEPT, YET I WOKE UP
IN SAFETY, FOR THE LORD WAS WATCHING
OVER ME.   *Psalm 3:5*

Traditions

MY QUESTION *for* GOD

How do spiritual traditions energize my faith?

A MOMENT *with* GOD

This is a day to remember. Each year, from
generation to generation, you must celebrate it as
a special festival to the LORD.   EXODUS 12:14

Watch out! Be careful never to forget what you
yourself have seen. Do not let these memories escape
from your mind as long as you live! And be sure to
pass them on to your children and grandchildren. . . .
Then they will learn to fear me as long as they live,
and they will teach their children to fear me also.

DEUTERONOMY 4:9-10

*G*od endorses traditions, especially those that have
spiritual significance. Traditions promote together-
ness and refresh your memories of God's faithfulness
to you by recalling how God has provided in the past.
The greatest inheritance you can provide for succeed-
ing generations are traditions that create divine moments to remind them frequently of God's blessings
and warnings. This rejuvenates their faith.

DIVINE PROMISE

YOUR FAITHFULNESS EXTENDS TO EVERY
GENERATION, AS ENDURING AS THE EARTH
YOU CREATED. *Psalm 119:90*

Trust

MY QUESTION *for* GOD

How can I know if God is trustworthy?

A MOMENT *with* GOD

God's way is perfect. All the LORD's promises
prove true. He is a shield for all who look to him for
protection.   PSALM 18:30

God can be trusted to keep his promise.   HEBREWS 10:23

The LORD is compassionate and merciful, slow to get
angry and filled with unfailing love.   PSALM 103:8

Your unfailing love, O LORD, is as vast as the
heavens; your faithfulness reaches beyond the clouds.
Your righteousness is like the mighty mountains, your
justice like the ocean depths. You care for people
and animals alike, O LORD. How precious is your
unfailing love, O God! All humanity finds shelter in
the shadow of your wings.   PSALM 36:5-7

*P*eople who consistently tell the truth are trustworthy;
you can count on them to do what they promise. How
much more trustworthy is the One who created truth,
who set the principles of moral law in motion? Therefore, God is not only truth*ful;* he *is* truth. Truth is not
just a character trait of God; it is the essence of who
he is. If truth comes from God, then he cannot lie or
renege on a promise he's made. It's impossible. What
God promises will always come true, and because he is

eternal, his truth will last forever. But God is also love. In the same way, love is not just a character trait of God but the essence of who he is. His love for you, therefore, is unconditional and can never be withdrawn. He loves you always. Because of God's unending truth and unfailing love, you can trust him completely when he says he has a plan for your life, that he wants to guide you to what is best for you: the place Jesus has prepared for you in heaven if you believe that he died for your sins and rose from the dead. Only when you understand how trustworthy God is can you walk in faith and let him lead you wherever he wants to take you. Suddenly, your fears for your future turn into an expectant adventure with God as your guide.

DIVINE PROMISE

JESUS CHRIST IS THE SAME YESTERDAY, TODAY, AND FOREVER.   *Hebrews 13:8*

Unity

MY QUESTIONS *for* GOD

How can I make peace with others? Is real unity possible?

A MOMENT *with* GOD

Make every effort to keep yourselves united in the Spirit, binding yourselves together with peace.

EPHESIANS 4:3

Search for peace, and work to maintain it.   PSALM 34:14

The body has many different parts, not just one part.

1 CORINTHIANS 12:14-20

*O*ne of the keys to unity is to celebrate one another's differences. Unity is not about everyone agreeing or having the same opinion. It's about learning how to take different opinions and direct them all toward a common purpose and goal. God creates everyone differently, so we should expect differences of opinion. But God also tells us to be united, which means that our differences must serve some important goal: bringing about the most thoughtful, well-developed plans. Unity usually becomes difficult to achieve when we're already convinced that our opinion is the best and therefore someone else's opinion is not well thought through. This mind-set keeps us from listening to new ideas that might actually make our own opinion better. Then we are in danger of "tuning out" a potential divine moment in which God helps us to see how different colors create a richer painting. Try celebrating and truly anticipating one another's differences and fitting them together to accomplish the objective. Then you will experience the true harmony and unity that God designed humans to share and enjoy.

DIVINE PROMISE

YOU ARE ALL CHILDREN OF GOD THROUGH
FAITH IN CHRIST JESUS. AND ALL WHO HAVE
BEEN UNITED WITH CHRIST IN BAPTISM
HAVE PUT ON CHRIST, LIKE PUTTING ON
NEW CLOTHES. THERE IS NO LONGER JEW OR
GENTILE, SLAVE OR FREE, MALE AND FEMALE.
FOR YOU ARE ALL ONE IN CHRIST JESUS.

Galatians 3:26-28

Victory

MY QUESTION *for* GOD

What are some victories I can achieve day by day?

A MOMENT *with* GOD

Abraham never wavered in believing God's promise.
In fact, his faith grew stronger, and in this he brought
glory to God.   ROMANS 4:20

These trials will show that your faith is genuine. It is
being tested as fire tests and purifies gold—though
your faith is far more precious than mere gold. So
when your faith remains strong through many trials,
it will bring you much praise and glory and honor on
the day when Jesus Christ is revealed to the whole
world.   1 PETER 1:7

I have discovered this principle of life—that when
I want to do what is right, I inevitably do what is
wrong. . . . Oh, what a miserable person I am! Who
will free me from this life that is dominated by sin

and death? Thank God! The answer is in Jesus Christ our Lord. So you see how it is: In my mind I really want to obey God's law, but because of my sinful nature I am a slave to sin.   ROMANS 7:21, 24-25

𝒜lthough your final victory over death is already assured if you have faith in Jesus, you still have to work for victory in the daily issues and temptations of life. You do this by obeying God in the little things: what you say, what you look at, how you react to others, what you think about, whether or not you tell the truth. It takes discipline to obey God each day as you face many small battles and temptations. But the more little battles you win, the more you experience peace in your life. Obedience to God steadies your heart, even in times of pain, confusion, loneliness, or distraction. It is in these weak moments that temptation strikes and defeats you. But steady obedience to God in the little things will give you daily victories that help strengthen your hope and endurance and bring greater peace of mind. With God's help, you can make progress every day. Today's victory is all you need for today. Take it one day at a time.

DIVINE PROMISE

VICTORY COMES FROM YOU, O LORD. MAY YOU BLESS YOUR PEOPLE. *Psalm 3:8*

Vision

MY QUESTIONS *for* GOD

How can I align my vision with God's plan for me? Why is it important for me to seek God's vision for the future?

A MOMENT *with* GOD

All glory to God, who is able, through his mighty power at work within us, to accomplish infinitely more than we might ask or think.   EPHESIANS 3:20

I tell you the truth, anyone who believes in me will do the same works I have done, and even greater works, because I am going to be with the Father.

JOHN 14:12

"My thoughts are nothing like your thoughts," says the LORD. "And my ways are far beyond anything you could imagine. For just as the heavens are higher than the earth, so my ways are higher than your ways and my thoughts higher than your thoughts."   ISAIAH 55:8-9

It has been said that "vision is a picture of the future that produces a passion in the present." Lack of vision is like trying to see underwater without a mask—everything is blurry, nothing makes sense, and you can feel impossibly lost. If you want a sharper picture of God's purpose for you, if you want to see more clearly your way in life, if you want to be motivated to do something that counts, you need vision—a picture of where you should be at some point in the future. Spiritual vision is God's picture of the future he created for you. How do you see God's picture of your future and purpose? You must fill yourself with God. You must get God in you. It's only when you empty yourself of your own opinions and dreams of the future that God can fill you up with his picture of the future. Only when you understand how filled with sin you are, experience brokenness about it, rid yourself of it, and fill yourself with God will you begin to know his vision. Seeking God's vision breaks your bondage to small ideas that are not worthy of God or representative of his work in the world. By aligning your vision with God's vision for your life, you will be able to navigate your future with purpose and clarity.

DIVINE PROMISE

NOW WE SEE THINGS IMPERFECTLY AS IN A CLOUDY MIRROR, BUT THEN WE WILL SEE EVERYTHING WITH PERFECT CLARITY.
1 Corinthians 13:12

Vulnerability

MY QUESTION *for* GOD

How can being vulnerable help me experience God?

A MOMENT *with* GOD

Have mercy on me, LORD, for I am in distress. Tears blur my eyes. My body and soul are withering away.

I am dying from grief; my years are shortened by
sadness. Sin has drained my strength; I am wasting
away from within.   PSALM 31:9-10

Come and listen to my counsel. I'll share my heart
with you and make you wise.   PROVERBS 1:23

If we confess our sins to him, he is faithful and just
to forgive us our sins and to cleanse us from all
wickedness.   1 JOHN 1:9

When you bare your soul to God in prayer, he reveals
himself to you. When you humbly and honestly release
your cares and admit your mistakes before God, he
softens your heart to hear his voice. God will also reveal to you truths and mysteries about himself and his
character. When you are honest with God, you open
the lines of genuine communication between you and
your Creator. Being vulnerable with God about your
sins and failures allows you to experience his absolute
faithfulness and forgiveness. You may often resist being honest with God about your sins—especially the
ones you don't want to give up—but vulnerability requires full disclosure, not hiding or covering up. It is
only through being vulnerable that you find true healing, restoration, renewal, and forgiveness. When you
acknowledge your sin, seek forgiveness, and commit
yourself to taking the high road, your relationship with
God is restored, and a great weight is lifted from you.

DIVINE PROMISE

THE LORD IS A FRIEND TO THOSE WHO FEAR
HIM. HE TEACHES THEM HIS COVENANT.
Psalm 25:14

Waiting

MY QUESTION *for* GOD

*I try to faithfully follow Jesus, so why does he often make me
wait for him to act?*

A MOMENT *with* GOD

The LORD your God will drive those nations out
ahead of you little by little. You will not clear them
away all at once, otherwise the wild animals would
multiply too quickly for you.

DEUTERONOMY 7:22

There is so much more I want to tell you, but you
can't bear it now.   JOHN 16:12

Be still in the presence of the LORD, and wait
patiently for him to act. Don't worry about evil
people who prosper or fret about their wicked
schemes.   PSALM 37:7

God always has your best interests at heart. But there
are times when delay may be better for you. As Israel
prepared for the conquest of the Promised Land, God
revealed that it would happen gradually because of the

need to preserve the balance of people and animals. In this case, God asked them to wait so that he could provide for them more abundantly. God often leads you to follow the path of progressive victory instead of immediate victory for your own protection and provision. Time spent waiting is never wasted by God, so don't waste it by being anxious. Even times of waiting can be divine moments when you learn to see how God is preparing you for the times ahead. As you wait for God to accomplish the next good thing in your life, don't be idle. Serve him where you are, and prepare yourself through spiritual training.

DIVINE PROMISE

AS FOR ME, I LOOK TO THE LORD FOR HELP.
I WAIT CONFIDENTLY FOR GOD TO SAVE ME,
AND MY GOD WILL CERTAINLY HEAR ME.
Micah 7:7

Will of God

MY QUESTION *for* GOD

Does God really have a plan for my life?

A MOMENT *with* GOD

The LORD says, "I will guide you along the best pathway for your life. I will advise you and watch over you."   PSALM 32:8

"I know the plans I have for you," says the LORD.
"They are plans for good and not for disaster, to give
you a future and a hope." JEREMIAH 29:11

You see me when I travel and when I rest at home.
You know everything I do. PSALM 139:3

Who knows if perhaps you were made queen for just
such a time as this? ESTHER 4:14

The LORD will work out his plans for my life.

PSALM 138:8

*T*hese Scripture verses, and many more, make it clear
that God does have a plan for your life. So how do you
know what it is and whether or not you are following it?
The first step is simply to accept the fact that God does
have a plan for you. Without this first step of faith, you
will miss everything God does to get your attention.
Next, open your eyes—your spiritual eyes. Notice the
people that come into your life, that cross your path
during the day. These may be people God wants to use
in your life or wants you to minister to. Act on what
and whom God places in front of you, and you will follow his plan for your life, day by day, month by month,
year by year. Your life will always have an element of
mystery, because you can't know the future. But if you
act on each situation God puts in front of you, your
life will not seem random, nor will it seem like an au-
tomated script you must follow. When you are always
watching for God's work in your life, you will train

yourself to notice these divine moments and recognize
them for what they are.

DIVINE PROMISE

**SEEK HIS WILL IN ALL YOU DO, AND HE WILL
SHOW YOU WHICH PATH TO TAKE.**   *Proverbs 3:6*

Wisdom

MY QUESTION *for* GOD

How can I be truly wise?

A MOMENT *with* GOD

Fear of the Lord is the foundation of wisdom.
Knowledge of the Holy One results in good
judgment.   PROVERBS 9:10

Don't lose sight of common sense and discernment.
Hang on to them, for they will refresh your soul.
They are like jewels on a necklace. They keep you
safe on your way, and your feet will not stumble.
You can go to bed without fear; you will lie down
and sleep soundly. You need not be afraid of sudden
disaster or the destruction that comes upon the
wicked, for the Lord is your security. He will
keep your foot from being caught in a trap.

PROVERBS 3:21-26

Anyone who listens to my teaching and follows it
is wise, like a person who builds a house on solid
rock. Though the rain comes in torrents and the
floodwaters rise and the winds beat against that
house, it won't collapse because it is built on bedrock.
But anyone who hears my teaching and doesn't
obey it is foolish, like a person who builds a house
on sand. When the rains and floods come and the
winds beat against that house, it will collapse with a
mighty crash.   MATTHEW 7:24-27

*W*isdom is more about who you know than what you
know. True wisdom begins with understanding your
accountability to and your full dependence on your
Creator and recognizing that he designed a moral
universe with consequences for your good and sinful
choices. Wisdom is more than simply knowing facts
and figures. Wisdom transforms head knowledge into
heartfelt action for good. Wisdom applies God's truth
and principles to your daily relationships and situations. It helps you to know the difference between
right and wrong, to choose what is right, and to avoid
the problems that come from wrong choices. Wisdom
from God helps you to penetrate the deceptions and
distortions the world throws at you. This worldview
helps you identify and communicate what is really true
and thus, make wiser decisions. The more you learn
to apply God's truth to everyday life, the more God's
wisdom will inspire your confidence and prepare you
for whatever happens to you in the future.

DIVINE PROMISE

TRUST IN THE LORD WITH ALL YOUR
HEART; DO NOT DEPEND ON YOUR OWN
UNDERSTANDING. SEEK HIS WILL IN ALL
YOU DO, AND HE WILL SHOW YOU WHICH
PATH TO TAKE. *Proverbs 3:5-6*

Work

MY QUESTION *for* GOD

How does knowing God transform my work?

A MOMENT *with* GOD

God created human beings in his own image. In the
image of God he created them; male and female he
created them. Then God blessed them and said, "Be
fruitful and multiply. Fill the earth and govern it.
Reign over the fish in the sea, the birds in the sky,
and all the animals that scurry along the ground."

GENESIS 1:27-28

On the seventh day God had finished his work of
creation, so he rested from all his work. . . . The
LORD God placed the man in the Garden of Eden to
tend and watch over it.   GENESIS 2:2, 15

As slaves of Christ, do the will of God with all your
heart. Work with enthusiasm, as though you were
working for the Lord rather than for people.

EPHESIANS 6:6-7

*K*nowing God gives added value to your work. God created people and gave them dominion over his Creation. In other words, God created you for work. Even when sin came into the world, humanity was given the opportunity to transform the raw materials of earth into things that would enhance life. Work has always been meant to honor God, to give people the dignity of having something important to do, and to bring blessings to others. But work is also anchored in God's character. Part of being made in God's image is sharing in the industrious and creative aspects of his nature. Christians are needed in all kinds of vocations. Whatever your job, believe that God has placed you there for a reason, and then do your work well as a service to God and as a way to allow others to see his love in action through you. The quality of your work and your enthusiasm for it reveal the nature of your commitment to Christ.

DIVINE PROMISE

WORK WILLINGLY AT WHATEVER YOU DO, AS THOUGH YOU WERE WORKING FOR THE LORD RATHER THAN FOR PEOPLE. REMEMBER THAT THE LORD WILL GIVE YOU AN INHERITANCE AS YOUR REWARD, AND THAT THE MASTER YOU ARE SERVING IS CHRIST. *Colossians 3:23-24*

Worship

MY QUESTION for GOD

Why is worship an important part of experiencing God?

A MOMENT with GOD

They know the truth about God because he has
made it obvious to them. For ever since the world
was created, people have seen the earth and sky.
Through everything God made, they can clearly see
his invisible qualities—his eternal power and divine
nature. So they have no excuse for not knowing God.

ROMANS 1:19-20

God is Spirit, so those who worship him must
worship in spirit and in truth.   JOHN 4:24

Oh, how great are God's riches and wisdom and
knowledge! How impossible it is for us to understand
his decisions and his ways! For who can know the
LORD's thoughts? Who knows enough to give him
advice? And who has given him so much that he needs
to pay it back? For everything comes from him and
exists by his power and is intended for his glory. All
glory to him forever! Amen.   ROMANS 11:33-36

All human beings were created to worship—to as-
cribe ultimate value to something or someone and then
to revere, adore, pay homage to, and obey by order-
ing the priorities of your life around what you worship. The Bible teaches that God alone is worthy of

your real worship and that worship, more than anything else, will connect you with God. You can connect with God in worship anytime, anyplace. It doesn't have to be confined to Sunday mornings in a church building. It honors God when you take time to praise him whenever you see his wisdom, power, direction, care, and love in your life. Worship then becomes a way of life, deepening your relationship with God and strengthening your ability to communicate with him. When you learn to worship as a way of life, you will find yourself experiencing divine moments with God more and more.

DIVINE PROMISE

YOU ARE WORTHY, O LORD OUR GOD, TO RECEIVE GLORY AND HONOR AND POWER. FOR YOU CREATED ALL THINGS, AND THEY EXIST BECAUSE YOU CREATED WHAT YOU PLEASED.

Revelation 4:11

Worth

MY QUESTION *for* GOD

How can I develop a healthier sense of self-worth?

A MOMENT *with* GOD

Be honest in your evaluation of yourselves, measuring yourselves by the faith God has given us.   ROMANS 12:3

God has given each of you a gift from his great variety
of spiritual gifts. Use them well to serve one another.

1 PETER 4:10

As for me, I look to the LORD for help. I wait
confidently for God to save me, and my God will
certainly hear me.   MICAH 7:7

A healthy sense of self-worth comes from an honest
balance between confidence and humility. The confidence comes from knowing that God created you
in his image and gifted you with special abilities. The
humility comes from knowing that without God you
would have nothing and be nothing. When you realize
that all you have is from God and that he created you
for a purpose, you can confidently exercise your gifts
and abilities for his glory. Maintaining this healthy balance between confidence and humility keeps you from
becoming too proud of your abilities and accomplishments or so self-effacing that you accomplish nothing.
Ultimately this balance is born out of a healthy relationship with God, your Creator. As you depend more
and more on him, he affirms your great value to him
and gives you the confidence and opportunities to be
productive for him.

DIVINE PROMISE
WE ARE GOD'S MASTERPIECE. HE HAS CREATED
US ANEW IN CHRIST JESUS, SO WE CAN DO
THE GOOD THINGS HE PLANNED FOR US
LONG AGO. *Ephesians 2:10*

Index

DIVINE
MOMENTS
Books

DIVINE
MOMENTS for
WOMEN
Everyday Inspiration
with God's Word

DIVINE
MOMENTS
Everyday Inspiration
from God's Word

DIVINE
MOMENTS for
MEN
Everyday Inspiration
from God's Word

DIVINE
MOMENTS for
STUDENTS
Everyday Inspiration
from God's Word

DIVINE
MOMENTS for
LEADERS
Everyday Inspiration
from God's Word

FEATURING THE
New Living
Translation

FEATURING THE
New Living
Translation

CP0196

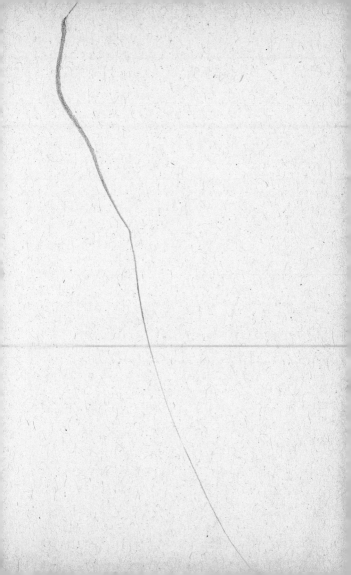